D0108267

Shared
Values
for a
Troubled
World

Foreword by Harlan Cleveland
Illustrations by Jo Spiller

Shared Values for a Troubled World

Conversations with Men and Women of Conscience

Rushworth M. Kidder

Jossey-Bass Publishers
San Francisco

Illustrations by Jo Spiller/Camden, Maine

Earlier versions of the interviews with Derek Bok, Kenneth Boulding, John W. Gardner, James Joseph, Graça Machel, and Reuben Snake appeared in the *Christian Science Monitor* and were used with permission from: © The Christian Science Publishing Society. All rights reserved.

Substantial discounts on bulk quantities of Jossey-Bass books are available to corporations, professional associations, and other organizations. For details and discount information, contact the special sales department at Jossey-Bass Inc., Publishers. (415) 433-1740; Fax (415) 433-0499.

For international orders, please contact your local Paramount Publishing International office.

Manufactured in the United States of America. Nearly all Jossey-Bass books, jackets, and periodicals are printed on recycled paper that contains at least 50 percent recycled waste, including 10 percent postconsumer waste. Many of our materials are also printed with vegetable-based ink; during the printing process these inks emit fewer volatile organic compounds (VOCs) than petroleum-based inks. VOCs contribute to the formation of smog.

Library of Congress Cataloging-in-Publication Data

Kidder, Rushworth M.
    Shared values for a troubled world: conversations with men and women of conscience / Rushworth M. Kidder.—1st ed.
        p.   cm.
    Includes index.
    ISBN 1-55542-603-4
    1. Ethics, Modern—20th century.   2. Values.   I. Title.
BJ319.K53   1994
170—dc20   93-33139
                                                                CIP

FIRST EDITION
HB Printing   10 9 8 7 6 5 4 3 2   Code 9420

Contents

•

Foreword

•

This book is so unusual as to be unique—a moral and intellectual safari around the world, in search of a global code of ethics.

Its presumption, in both senses of the word, is that there are some values so universal to the human mind, so fundamental to the human spirit, that they transcend the boundaries that sacred text and secular philosophies have created to protect differing cultural identities.

Rushworth Kidder is president of the Institute for Global Ethics, a longtime columnist for the *Christian Science Monitor*, and a perceptive reporter and thoughtful analyst with vast experience in tracking worldwide political, economic, and cultural trends. This work caused him to worry about "a global breakdown in ethics and morality," led him to found a think tank focused on global ethics, and motivated him to travel far and wide in search of insight and inspiration.

He has crossed bloody ethnic frontiers, deep intellectual divides, yawning cultural chasms, and wide valleys of doctrinal dispute and misunderstanding. Now and again he identified some special people, people with critical minds and unusually clear ideas about their values.

His search took him around the world to talk with a Maori wise woman, a Buddhist monk, a Vietnamese activist, a Polish-Canadian environmentalist, a Native-American tribal chief, an Afro-American foundation executive, Mozambique's former first lady, a former president of Harvard, an Oxford don, an Australian author, an unorthodox banker in Bangladesh, a unique economics professor, a top U.S. business executive, a communications lawyer, an American public philosopher, a Chinese author, a Sri Lankan journalist, a Swedish author, an Hispanic editor, a British columnist, a Nobel Laureate in Costa Rica, a former prime minister of Lebanon, a U.S. ambassador to the United Nations, and the director general of UNESCO.

Interviews with these twenty-four people—thinkers with the courage to express their thoughts in action, activists who think hard about why they act—are pulled together in this book. But, fascinating though these people are in themselves, this is no miscellany of journalistic encounters. Their thoughts are collected between two covers to see whether there is a common ground of values that could bring the world's peoples together instead of driving them apart.

From this small universe of two dozen wise but not omniscient individuals, talking about the values each considers the fundament of his or her philosophy, Rushworth Kidder derives a draft global code of ethics—a body of useful ideas, universal and therefore somehow unsurprising. Some are recognizable in the sacred texts of every world religion. Some are to be found in such secular texts as the American Declaration of Independence, the French Declaration of the Rights of Man, and in our own time, the Universal Declaration of Human Rights (1948), and the Helsinki Final Act (1975).

Is a universe of twenty-four men and women, even a group so diverse by culture and geography, an adequate sample of what the American founding fathers called "the general opinion of mankind?"

Pollsters undertake to tell us what we collectively think and feel after interviewing a thousand or so out of nearly a quarter of a billion people. Clerics of competing religious traditions assure us that the wisdom of one special man— Jesus, or Mohammed, or the Gautama Buddha—is all we really need to know to be saved.

The author of this book does not pretend to present either a scientific sample or a prophetic vision. But these thoughtful and articulate people, their views and their values captured and capsuled by a skillful interviewer, may have as good a chance as a cast of thousands replying to a pollster's queries, or even a lone prophet speaking from the heart, to come up with a set of universal maxims for our time on this earth.

Most of these interviewees would wave off with a self-deprecating smile any presumption of prophetic vision. Yet in one-on-one conversations with an ethical mixmaster of Rush Kidder's quality, each is lured into visionary prophecy.

The global code of ethics that emerges from the blender
has to be taken very seriously.

It is not, as the author keeps reminding us, *the* answer.
But it is *an* answer to the primordial question about the
twenty-first century: Can we, the world's peoples, come together on ethical common ground that doesn't permit the
human experiment to end with either a bang *or* a whimper?

Minneapolis, Minnesota   Harlan Cleveland
January 1994   *President*
                    World Academy of Art and Science

Preface

•

If this book had a beginning, I suppose it came in the fall
of 1986 when, as a senior columnist for the *Christian Science
Monitor*, I began interviewing twenty-two leading global
citizens to discover the half-dozen major, first-intensity,
make-it-or-break-it issues on the twenty-first century's
agenda. I had expected to hear about five problems that, in
the end, did indeed figure strongly on our list: the nuclear
threat, environmental degradation, the population crisis, the
North-South gap between haves and have-nots, and the
need for education reform. But I was unprepared for the
force with which another issue came onto the agenda. When
the newspaper series (and subsequently the book, *An
Agenda for the 21st Century*) was published, its pages were
full of references to that sixth item: the pervasive concern
about a global breakdown in ethics and morality.

In his presidential villa in Bonn, West Germany, Richard
von Weizsäcker spoke fervently of the need for an "ethics

of living, individually and socially." From his living room in suburban Tokyo, Japanese philosopher Suichi Kato talked of a society so blunted in its moral sensitivities that it was "not very much concerned, seriously, with other people's suffering."

Over breakfast in London, Mexican novelist Carlos Fuentes urged attention to "the moral rewards of progress"; over mid-morning coffee in his kitchen in Aspen, Colorado, philosopher Mortimer Adler spoke of the "moral and intellectual responsibilities" of democracy; at her home in Cambridge, Massachusetts, philosopher Sissela Bok predicted that, to survive the twenty-first century, government leaders would need to "take moral principles into account" in their decision making.

And so it went. In conversations with some of the world's more thoughtful individuals, this topic bubbled to the surface. Right up alongside the nuclear threat and the degradation of the environment, they put their worry about a meltdown of the core moral values by which people live. Why such concern? Because an ethical collapse, they seemed to be saying, could undo us just as forcefully, and nearly as quickly, as any of the other five issues they identified.

Shared Values for a Troubled World is an effort to explore that sixth point. Through a series of interviews, it sets out to address this problem in a positive and solution-oriented way. It begins with a single question: if there could be a global code of ethics, what would it contain?

Why is a book on this subject needed? Because ethics is rapidly becoming as much a survival issue as the other five—a contention I develop in the opening chapter and which many of the interviewees support. It is also needed because, unlike the other five issues, ethics has yet to establish itself as a domain of domestic and foreign affairs that brings policy analysts, journalists, teachers, diplomats, and the public together with a common mindset and stance. The need, ultimately, is for a language of public discourse that lets us talk broadly about ethics without sounding vacuous or Victorian—a language which, I hope, this book helps develop.

By the very nature of its subject matter, then, this book is not only for experts. To be sure, many of the voices assembled here are specialists in their own fields. But the subject upon which they are speaking—the possibility of creating a code of shared values for a troubled and fragmenting world—is so broad that it demands of them a fresh and general language. As such, the book ought to be of interest to anyone concerned about humanity's ethical barometer, worried about the place of values in what sometimes seems a values-free society, and interested in relating the world's moral future to educational, corporate, academic, governmental, or professional settings. In other words, it ought to interest anyone wanting to find ways to create a sustainable twenty-first century.

Overview of the Contents

The first chapter lays the groundwork by asking why we need, more than ever, a core of shared values—and whether we can in fact find such a thing.

Chapter Two brings together those individuals whose

focus has been on religion, philanthropy, and charitable activities: Native-American tribal chief Reuben Snake, foundation executive James A. Joseph, Buddhist monk Shojun Bando, Vietnamese writer and activist Le Ly Hayslip, and Father Bernard Przewozny, administrator of an international environmental prize.

Chapter Three, embracing education and youth, includes Mozambique's former first lady Graça Machel, former Harvard University president Derek Bok, New Zealand Maori activist Dame Whina Cooper, Oxford don A. H. Halsey, and Australian author and former Smith College president Jill Ker Conway.

In Chapter Four, where the concentration is on business and the economy, the individuals include Bangladeshi banker Muhammad Yunus, British-born economist and author Kenneth Boulding, American chief executive officer James K. Baker, former Federal Communications Commission chairman Newton Minow, and John W. Gardner, founder of the citizen lobbying organization Common Cause.

Chapter Five is given over to authors and journalists: Chinese author Nien Cheng, whose *Life and Death in Shanghai* was a best-seller in the United States; Sri Lankan journalist and former United Nations official Tarzie Vittachi; Swedish author Astrid Lindgren; Hispanic columnist and editor Sergio Muñoz; and Katharine Whitehorn, columnist for the *Observer* (London).

Chapter Six, which concentrates on political leadership, brings together the former head of state of Costa Rica and Nobel Laureate Oscar Arias; Salim El Hoss, former Prime Minister of Lebanon; former U.S. ambassador to the United

Nations Jeane Kirkpatrick; and Federico Mayor, director-general of UNESCO.

The final chapter draws out an eight-point code of values that arises from these interviews.

Acknowledgments

Because this book depends so heavily on a proper selection of individuals to be interviewed, I owe voluminous debts to friends and acquaintances whom I solicited—and sometimes badgered—for potential names, and who gave me several hundred thoughtful, well-considered suggestions. While these recommenders are too many to be listed, the following must be mentioned: Marjorie Allen, James K. Baker, Wendell Bell, Sissela Bok, Rodrigo Botero, Harlan Cleveland, Katherine Fanning, John Gardner, Karl Gerstenberger, Theodore J. Gordon, Willard Hanzlik, Kristin Helmore, True and Ewen Henderson, Michael K. Hooker, Gladys and Clayton Jones, James A. Joseph, George Moffett, Bill Moyers, Olusegun Obasanjo, Robert Payton, Peter Raven, Randa M. Slim, Theodore Taylor, William S. White, Katharine Whitehorn, Anna Lena Wik-Thorsell, and Daniel Yankelovich. I also owe a great deal of thanks to the following staff and associates at the Institute for Global Ethics, a nonprofit think tank launched several years ago in Camden, Maine, for sustaining this project: Patricia Born Brousseau, Betcie Byrd, Barton W. Emanuel, Paula Fenton, Carl Hausman, Carol Shaw, Melody Smith, Jo Spiller, and Robert Tierney.

I must thank, too, the interviewees themselves. They came to this project from a variety of backgrounds and view-points, but they saw enough of its significance to give it their time and attention. More than that, they gave it their inspiration. Again and again, as I talked with these exceptional individuals, I was impressed by the extent to which they had prepared themselves for my visit by organizing their ideas into coherent streams and orderly steps. When on occasion they thanked me for impelling them to think about ethics in such detail, I could only rebound the thanks to them. They, after all, are what this book is all about.

I am greatly indebted to the W. K. Kellogg Foundation for its generous support of this specific project, to the Flora and John Schumann Foundation and the Charles Stewart Mott Foundation for early support of the institute, and to the numerous individuals who, by becoming members of the Institute for Global Ethics, have helped this project. Finally, I am profoundly grateful for the help and counsel of my wife, Elizabeth, whose high ethical standards and clear insights into character have shaped this book in ways beyond recounting, and to whom it is dedicated.

Lincolnville, Maine   Rushworth M. Kidder
January 1994   *President*
                                    The Institute for Global Ethics

The Author

•

Rushworth M. Kidder, President of the Institute for Global Ethics, has been a foreign correspondent, editor, and senior columnist for the *Christian Science Monitor*, an international daily newspaper highly regarded for its depth, balance, and ethical stance. Before joining the paper, Kidder spent ten years as a professor of English at Wichita State University in Kansas.

An honors graduate of Amherst College, he earned his M.A. and Ph.D. degrees from Columbia University in English and comparative literature. The author of seven books, including the award-winning *E. E. Cummings: An Introduction to the Poetry* (1979), his work has also appeared in the American Society of Newspaper Editors' *Best Newspaper Writing, 1983*. The *New York Times* has described Kidder as one of the *Monitor's* "most celebrated journalists." He has written major series for the *Monitor* on such subjects as international terrorism, quantum mechanics, and the state of marriage in America, and is well known among futurists for his books *An Agenda for the 21st Century* (1987) and *Reinventing the Future: Global Goals for the 21st Century* (1989).

In 1990, Kidder founded the Institute for Global Ethics in Camden, Maine, a membership-based nonprofit organization which examines ethical issues in an international context. Through its monthly periodicals, seminars, conferences, and publications, the institute seeks to provide practical approaches to resolving contemporary ethical dilemmas.

He and his wife, Elizabeth, have two daughters and live in Lincolnville, Maine.

*Shared
Values
for a
Troubled
World*

ONE

Uncovering Our Universal Values

*I think this is a long, slow exploration to
discover common ground.*

—John W. Gardner

In the remote New Zealand village of Panguru, tucked into
the mountains at the end of a winding gravel road, a Maori
woman nearly a century old pauses for a moment as she
talks about the moral values of her people. "This is God's
country!" says Dame Whina Cooper with great feeling, gesturing toward the flowers blooming among the bird songs

outside her modest frame house. "Only, we the people running it must be doing something wrong."

Halfway around the world, in a United Nations office perched under the eaves of a fifteenth-century building in Florence, a leading journalist from Sri Lanka is asked what will happen if the world enters the twenty-first century with the ethics of the twentieth century. "I feel it will be disastrous," Tarzie Vittachi replies simply.

Midway between, in his well-appointed residence in San Jose, Costa Rica, former president Oscar Arias explains that our global survival "will be a more complicated and precarious question than ever before, and the ethics required of us must be correspondingly sophisticated."

In Washington, Chinese author Nien Cheng speaks of "a moral crisis" in her homeland. In Stockholm, Swedish children's writer Astrid Lindgren observes that the values of today's children make them "a strange lot of people." In Tokyo, a Buddhist monk named Shojun Bando calls the worsening ethical climate in Japan "so serious that it's unprecedented." In Chicago, American lawyer Newton Minow identifies "the dominant characteristic" of modern society as "an unwillingness to confront what we regard as evil, or wrong, and say so." In California, Vietnamese author Le Ly Hayslip notes that "when you're talking about the global getting along or not getting along, we're too much separated. We don't understand the basic need."

Turn where you will in the world, it seems, and the refrain is the same: the ethical barometer is falling, and the consequences appear to be grave. That, at least, is one of the impressions to be drawn from the twenty-four individuals from sixteen nations interviewed in these pages.

This is not a book about the ethical failings of various nations. It's about the moral glue that binds us together as a world. But in the course of the interviews that follow, so many voices from so many different backgrounds have spoken so earnestly about the world's moral situation that their warnings can't be brushed aside. Something, they are saying, is profoundly and globally amiss, not just economically, or militarily, or politically, but ethically. Something deep in the soul of our collective future seems out of balance, and the world appears to be in a long, slow drift toward moral recession.

Yet just as powerfully, these voices speak of an underlying moral presence shared by all humanity—a set of precepts so fundamental that they dissolve borders, transcend races, and outlast cultural traditions. English scholar and author A. H. Halsey, from his office at Oxford University, calls it "a moral dimension" that permeates all of human activity. Father Bernard Przewozny, from his monastery outside of Rome, speaks of "certain absolute norms." Stanford University's John Gardner simply calls it "common ground."

"Everybody—I don't care what color, creed, ethnic origin their roots are—we're all the same," says American Indian tribal leader Reuben Snake from his home on the Winnebago Reservation in Nebraska. "In spite of all of these technological achievements, we're beginning to understand that there is a oneness to the whole universe."

That oneness, for many, rests on underlying moral values, a kind of global code of ethics neither invented or imposed, but rather discovered and identified. Federico Mayor, the director-general of the United Nations Educational, Scientific, and Cultural Organization (UNESCO), describes these values as "the spiritual heritage and patrimony that is the only thing that can give cohesion to our prospects for the future." Or, as Sergio Muñoz, former editor of the Los Angeles Spanish-language daily newspaper *La Opinion* explains, "It really doesn't matter whether you are Muslim or Christian or Jew. In every religion, in every country, in every region at every time, there are some basic principles."

"If you look at virtually all the civilizations that we have had over the past few centuries," says former Harvard University president Derek Bok, "one does find disagreements on details, but a remarkable consensus on certain basic, ethical precepts which form the foundation for a serious ethical code." And while there may be serious debate about just what the code contains, he adds, "the zone of agreement is vast. We're arguing about exactly where the borderline is in a few fringe areas."

Yet so tenacious are those arguments that the world seems in danger of coming unstuck over the assumption—for that's all it is—that no core of common values really exists. Nowhere are those arguments more vehemently asserted than in educational institutions when the question of teaching ethics arises. There, again and again, those concerns typically reduce themselves to a stinging five-word refrain meant to squelch all further discussion: *Whose ethics will you teach?*

Whose ethics will you teach? As the twenty-first century

4

approaches, that's among the most important questions we face as a global society. Why? Because it speaks directly to our future, our willingness to help our children create a world of effective and compassionate relationships, our ability to sustain ourselves as a human community. It's a variant, after all, of the time-worn question from which so much metaphysical inquiry springs: *What values will you live by?*

It's also a question that resounds far beyond the ivied walls of the university. Neither professors nor researchers have a corner on the answers. Each of us, after all, is a teacher of moral values. The examples we set, the choices we make, the lives we live broadcast potent, clear ethical signals to all within our radius. We cannot avoid responsibility for our moral atmosphere. We create it hour by hour in our actions and motives, seeding the next generation of moral actions with the ones we cultivate as models today.

That, of course, is not new. Every generation has asked, "Whose values?" And every generation has recognized that, intentionally or not, values are steadily being taught, either for better or for worse. As we move into the next century, however, this question burns with increasing brightness. It's not that values are suddenly more practical, more popular, or more pervasive than they once were. It's simply that the best vision we have of our global tomorrow presents us with three central trends—worldshrink, technobulge, and the need for consensus building—that will make our future qualitatively different from our past.

• *Worldshrink.* It's no secret that twenty-first-century pressures of population, communication, and economics will

5

produce requirements for global interdependence unimaginable in earlier ages. It's already obvious, for example, that the global media, by spreading the story of starvation and overcrowding in Africa and of ethnic ferocity in former East-bloc countries, has given the developed nations an entirely new impetus for military intervention. That impetus is not based on the old chestnuts of national interests or strategic defenses or mercantile concerns. It's based quite simply on the new politics of humanitarianism: we intervene because we see it as the morally right thing to do, even though it registers none of the standard benefits on the abacus of national self-interest.

Equally apparent is the fact that, because of the ease of long-distance travel that makes such intervention possible, every nation is increasingly blessed with cadres of experts and lay persons who have "been there"—wherever the latest "there" happens to be—and who no longer think of "there" as quite so foreign as it once was. Add to that the international movements of capital and a burgeoning export and import trade, and it's clear that we are seeing a blurring of national borders and a thirst to comprehend the cultures, tastes, manners, and attitudes of customers, clients, and friends all across the world.

As this worldshrink continues, there will be few havens from international crosscurrents, few backwaters where small groups can make a separate peace with overarching global forces. We will become, as Marshall McLuhan rightly foresaw, a global village—a community bound to interact with itself at every level. But as John Gardner observes in the following pages, "common ground emerges when a community is formed," and, conversely, a community, almost by definition, requires a shared ethic. Without a common set of values, communities are no more than unstable collections of individuals coexisting uneasily within common boundaries. It may not be too much to say, then, that our very survival as a global community will depend on our shared ethic. It will depend, in other words, on our willingness to identify and come together around a core of common values that allows us to interact successfully. Without that common ground, we risk being a community only in name, experiencing an ever-increasing intensity of interaction, but lacking the agreement on central values that makes coexistence possible.

• *Technobulge.* As the world shrinks, however, technology expands. As a result, today's ethical issues are not only different in scale from those of our ancestors. They are different in kind—and far more complex. When President Harry Truman dropped the atom bomb on Hiroshima on August 6, 1945, he ushered in an entirely new range of ethical decisions. Never before had there been such a weapon of mass destruction. Never before had humanity needed to contemplate the possibility of global holocaust. Never before had a single technology spawned such moral concern, with fears of a nuclear winter boiling over into a global peace movement that spanned any number of languages and reached from salons and seminars to tee shirts and bumper stickers. And never before had such a bevy of nuclear technologies—in such areas as medical treatment and electric-power generation—spun off such an array of conundrums concern-

7

ing side effects and waste disposal. Overnight, with the onset of Hiroshima and its grisly retinue, the moral responsibilities of world leadership ratcheted upward.

Yet the moral imperatives of a nuclear age may soon pale beside the ethical dilemmas raised by the Human Genome Project. Still in its youth, the project has already yielded groundbreaking technologies for embryonic diagnosis and genetic mapping. It is now possible to extract a single cell from a days-old human embryo and examine it for disease-promoting genes. Just over the horizon lies the capacity to reconstruct the genetic content of that same embryo to make it perform properly. But what does "perform properly" mean, and who decides? Should the technology be used only to repair bad embryos, or to make good ones better? Could it be perverted into efforts to create superior intellects among some children and a slave-race mentality among others? And what about your own right to genetic privacy in the face of demands by employers and insurance firms, who would dearly like to know whether you are more at risk of contracting an "expensive" disease down the road than someone else applying for the same job?

Beyond radiation and genetics lies a technological frontier that may, in the end, have an even greater daily effect on us: weather control. Here, too, the technologies raise such pressing moral issues that even meteorologists may someday face Trumanesque decisions. Using sophisticated cloud-seeding techniques, they may be able to trick tropical storms into exhausting themselves early, before making land. But seeding could also cause them to change course unpredictably. And therein lies just one of the many ethical challenges related to weather control. Suppose you could have seeded Andrew, the hurricane that devastated parts of south Florida and Louisiana in the summer of 1992. But suppose you also knew that the seeding might have made it strike not Homestead and the Everglades but central Miami and its vast population—or even Cuba and its annoyingly communist rulers. Would you have done it?

These points aren't raised to inveigh against technology. That would be futile. In these and a host of other areas, the genie is out of the bottle and can't be squeezed back in. The argument, instead, is for an ethical wisdom to match our technological prowess.

• *Consensus building.* The third reason to pay attention to the "Whose values?" question centers on the necessity for problem solving. The approach of the new millennium, like the onset of New Year's Day and its resolutions, is already inspiring deep soul-searching about where we've been and where we're going. As the century ends, the prospect of an uncertain, complex, and fragmented future impels a heightened search for points of moral stability as platforms for problem solving.

And problems do indeed abound, made all the more compelling by the pressures of worldshrink and technobulge. Worldshrink persuades us that the wholeness we yearn for cannot be local or regional: too many issues, from famine and the economy to education and the environment, are so globally interlocked as to require a holistic approach. Technobulge persuades us that our technologies are so large that they can easily leverage single moral decisions into globe-wrenching proportions—whether the decision site be the Oval Office before the bomb was dropped on Hiroshima, or the bridge of the *Exxon Valdez* before it ran aground in Alaska under the nondirection of a drunken captain, or the control room of Reactor Number Four at Chernobyl minutes before an ill-conceived experiment blew the roof off. Both worldshrink and technobulge hand us a sobering realization: there is no decision you could have wished onto a nineteenth-century president, no ethical lapse you could have found in a nineteenth-century sea captain, no power plant you could have turned over to a couple of nineteenth-century engineers that could have had the massive effects of their modern, high-tech-driven counterparts.

The point? Simply that we need problem solving as never before. That's not an exaggeration. In the past, humanity's safety valve was fabricated from a combination of diversity and isolation. Diversity argued that if one nation destroyed itself through inner turmoil, outward slaughter, and a general moral collapse, another somewhere else would be sane enough to survive and perpetuate the human species. Isolation further argued that such destruction, however appalling, would be contained: even while the Roman Empire was spiraling downward toward the sack of Rome by the Visigoths in 410 A.D., the Mesoamerican civilization of the Teotihuacan Empire was busily flourishing, and China was about to enter its great era. Now, with isolation fading and diversity threatened, the problems facing one nation press in upon all, brought home all the more forcefully in the lurid light of satellite-bounced television signals in our living rooms. Global problem solving, once considered a luxury reserved for those who could afford to think grand thoughts, has now become a concern for anyone who thinks at all. It has become, to put it simply, essential to our survival.

But real problem solving always comes with a prerequisite: a common framework of values, explicit or unarticulated, in which all parties to the solution feel some ownership. Global problem solving, in particular, requires a shared set of values, common not only across the different disciplines and skills needed around the table but across the different cultures, races, and traditions involved in the solution. Only if global problem solving arises from a consensus on a core of values will its premises be acceptable and its conclusions doable.

So which values do you teach? If you're concerned about worldshrink, you'll teach the ones that help turn collections of isolated individuals into genuine communities. If you're concerned about technobulge, you'll teach the ones that most help us cope with the moral dilemmas raised by a complex new set of technologies. And if you're concerned about consensus building, you'll teach the ones that are so commonplace, so simply grasped, and so universally applicable that they have direct relevance not only to policy elites and academic gurus but to every individual who feels in his or her own life a yearning to do and to be good.

•

"Yes, but," the cynics splutter, "what if there *are* no common values? What if the question, 'Whose values will you teach?' is simply a way of reminding us that we *really don't have* any shared ethic?"

Fair enough. Looking around the world, one could be forgiven for thinking that humanity is not, in fact, living in accordance with any fixed ethical principles. Again and again the news media call our attention to ethical lapses—in private life and in government, sports, the professions, the media, business, and in a host of other areas. In the past several years alone, any number of American household names, from financier Ivan Boesky to evangelists Jim and Tammy Bakker, have been tossed up on the shores of ethical turpitude. The moral driftwood from other nations—from Japanese power broker Shin Kanemaru, disgraced in a major scandal over political donations and links to organized crime, to Michael Garretta, the former head of France's national blood bank who was convicted in 1992 of knowingly dispensing AIDS-tainted blood for transfusions in the mid-1980s—is equally sobering.

As though to spotlight the problems, international opinion-leaders are increasingly pointing to ethics as one of the major, first-intensity issues of the future. In a twenty-nation 1989 survey of over 1,500 executives by Korn/Ferry International and the Columbia University School of Business, "personal ethics" topped a list of characteristics needed by the ideal corporate leader in the year 2000. "My experience as the leader of the intellectual organization of the United Nations," reports Federico Mayor in the pages that follow, "is that today, more than ever, ethics is at the very, very forefront of the world preoccupation as we approach the next millennium."

12

In the United States, at least, there is reason for their preoccupation. In a July 1991 survey of almost sixteen thousand students at thirty-one top American universities by Professor Donald McCabe of Rutgers University, 76 percent of those pursuing graduate degrees in business admitted to having cheated at least once on a test while an undergraduate. That figure squares with other similarly discouraging polling data: a survey done by the Louis Harris organization for the Girl Scouts found that when you ask high schoolers in the United States, "Would you cheat to pass an important exam?" two-thirds say, "Yes." When Shearson-Lehman polled the yuppie set, they found that nearly 40 percent of eighteen-to-twenty-nine-year-olds felt that corruption and deceit were important ways of getting ahead in the world. And when, in 1992, the Gallup Organization dipped into the attitudes Americans hold toward other Americans, they found that two-thirds were "unhappy with the honesty and ethical standards of other citizens."

There is, then, ample reason to want to teach a core of moral values—if only they could be found. We have, apparently, failed in our efforts to reach a consistently high set of ethical standards. But failing to reach standards is a very different thing from having no standards to reach. Are there, in fact, no standards out there, despite what wise men and women tell us?

The belief that no objective moral standards are to be found in the universe—a concept that so often underpins the challenge voiced in the question, "But whose ethics will you teach?"—has such a long and well-rehearsed background that it deserves some attention here. The idea is firmly established in certain quarters that there can be no agreed-upon standards of right and wrong. It insists that no one can lay down common principles, or even accurately assess another's values. It argues that, at bottom, all forms of behavior must be tolerated, since there are no fixed precepts upon which to base our values and therefore no way to condemn or even dispute the moral basis for behavior. It insists that everything that passes for ethics is really only a situational, negotiated response to a world that is fluid, mutable, and subjective. And it demands that all education be rigorously—one might almost have said *religiously*—values-neutral.

This relativism is hardly new, though it has only recently become widely acceptable. While it has profound roots in academic discourses on philosophy, it finally reached public thought in the early twentieth-century—traceable, some scholars say, to misinterpretations of Einstein's theory of relativity. Confirmed in 1919, Einstein's theory seized the imagination of a public not always capable of understanding its complexities and limitations. "At the beginning of the 1920s," writes British historian Paul Johnson, "the belief began to circulate, for the first time at a popular level, that there were no longer any absolutes: of time and space, of good and evil, of knowledge, above all of value. Mistakenly but perhaps inevitably, relativity became confused with relativism" (p. 4).* Coupled with the theses advanced by Freud and Marx, writes Johnson, this concept of relativism helped to "undermine . . . the highly developed sense of

* *Modern Times: The World from the Twenties to the Eighties.* New York: Harper-Collins, 1983.

personal responsibility, and of duty towards a settled and objectively true moral code, which was at the centre of nineteenth-century European civilization." The result, Johnson concludes, was a "vision . . . of moral anarchy" (p. 11).*

To be fair, such relativism was not all bad. In the name of tolerance, it erected a useful barrier against the kind of hortatory and intrusive self-righteousness that so often sought, in earlier ages as well as in certain militant fundamentalist sectors of today's world, to impose its moral values on others. It also reflected our age's deep and noble desire to respect diversity. At heart, however, the doctrine of relativism shrivels into intellectual unsoundness. Its rallying cry—that there are no absolutes—is often so vehemently asserted as to become an absolute itself. Its dogma promotes a disregard for shared commitments, encourages the dissolution of standards of action, and replaces a disciplined desire to distinguish worth with a wholesale acceptance of "whatever turns you on." It dilutes the capacity to defer gratification and build for the future. And its adoption as an educational standard makes it nearly impossible to promulgate ethical ideas among succeeding generations: if there is no fixed moral ground, where does one stand to teach?

The task for the twenty-first century, as it moves into global interrelatedness, will be to steer a middle course between standards and tolerance. No one is arguing for a return to the kind of nineteenth-century colonial culture where rigid standards swept aside any possible tolerance of different values. Yet neither should we be arguing for an abolition of all standards in a flaccid reverence for diversity.

The task of the twenty-first century will be to discover the common ethic that reflects an appreciation for sound standards while retaining the tremendous progress we have made in many areas toward tolerance and diversity.

•

There is, then, a pressing need for shared values in an age of worldshrink, technobulge, and failures of consensus. There is also, it would seem, little reason to assume that moral relativism is equal to the task of building a sustainable future. But to press the case for shared values, and to counter the relativist's arguments against finding them, still leaves one very practical question unanswered: is there *in fact* a set of values that wise, ethical people around the world might agree on? Can there be a global code of ethics? If there is a common core of values "out there" in the world, it ought to be identifiable through examination of contemporary modes of thought in various cultures around the world. Can it be found?

On that topic, this book has a clear point of view. "Yes," it says, "there is such a code, and it can be clearly articulated." The chapters that follow comprise interviews with ethical thought leaders from different cultures. They have been chosen not because they necessarily know more about ethics than their peers—although some do, having made it a lifelong study. Nor have they been chosen because they are the single most exemplary person of their nation or community—though some could easily be nominated for that honor. They represent businessmen, tribal leaders, political figures, theologians, authors, and teachers. They include women and men, liberals and conservatives, whites and non-whites. They include a variety of religious persuasions. They include some of worldwide renown, and—given the fact that eminence and ethics don't always keep company together—others revered only within their own neighborhoods.

But the individuals whose voices are heard here all have this in common: each is to some extent viewed by his or her peers as an ethical standard-bearer, a keeper of the conscience of their community, a center of moral gravity. They were selected only after considerable discussion and debate with my colleagues at the Institute for Global Ethics, where most of the work on this book has been done, and with friends and contacts in other parts of the world over the last four years. They don't think of themselves as paragons of virtue, and I would certainly not want to portray them as the only beacons of ethical light that could be found. Our drawers are full, in fact, of the names of hundreds of people who could have been interviewed—an encouraging file for those who, like Diogenes, would go about with a candle seeking honesty in the moral twilight.

Each of these interviews, which typically lasted at least an hour, was conducted face-to-face and recorded on audiotape. Each began with a common question: if you could help create a global code of ethics, what would be on it? What moral values, in other words, would you bring to the table from your own culture and background? Further discussion elicited examples of the ethical concerns these individuals found paramount in their lives and experiences,

along with comments on the state of the world's moral barometer and on directions that individuals and nations might
take to create a more ethical future.

Those conversations became the basis for the interviews
that follow. They are grouped according to the backgrounds
and interests of the interviewees—a loose grouping, to be
sure, since so many of these individuals move in so many
different circles.

The five chapters that follow record the voices of individuals around the world, chosen for their ethical sensibili-
ties, who speak out of five broad areas of human experience:
religion and charity, education and the future of our youth,
entrepreneurship and activism in business and economics,
literature and journalism, and government and politics.

The concluding chapter analyzes the common threads
and draws out the shared elements that form a global code
of ethics. What's on that code? Since this book is not a
thriller whose ending must be kept secret, the list can be
shared now—and, perhaps, chewed over and digested by
the reader as the interviews themselves unfold. The code
consists of eight moral values that will shape our global future in the next century and beyond:

- Love
- Truthfulness
- Fairness
- Freedom
- Unity
- Tolerance

- Responsibility
- Respect for life

So what values will you teach? This book gives, if not *the* answer, at least *an* answer. It offers for consideration—and certainly for departure and refinement—a set of values that is simple, direct, and fairly universal. It provides, in other words, a code so basic and widespread that the concern about "Whose values?" fades into a recognition of "Our values"—the ones articulated by wise and thoughtful people around the world who, in the pages that follow, have no agenda to pursue other than helping create the moral conditions for a sustainable twenty-first century.

TWO

Religion and Charity
The Search for Beginnings

*The search for common grounds begins with
the search for beginnings.*

—James A. Joseph

Reuben Snake

Intuitive Thinking in a High-Tech Age

*The Indian is a part of the creation, and
we're supposed to fit into and be harmonious
with the creation, and not to have the thought
that we can dominate any part of it.*

Ask LaDonna Harris about Reuben Snake, and she zeros in on his commitment to ethics.

American Indians have "just recently gotten to a position of articulating our values in terms of a Western context," says Ms. Harris, a Commanche who is president of the Washington-based Americans for Indian Opportunity. Snake, she says, was "more able to do that than anyone I know."

Eddy Tullis, tribal chairman of the Poarch Creek Indians of Alabama and chairman of several national committees on Indian issues, notes that he probably had "the most broad-based involvement in Indian activities of anyone in the country." He calls Snake "a very ethical person, a very spiritual person, well-informed, and well-involved."

That involvement began early. Born on the Winnebago Reservation in Nebraska, Snake grew up in Iowa, Wisconsin, Minnesota, and Kansas, attending mission schools and a federal boarding school. In 1965, he returned to Indian issues through the radical American Indian Movement (AIM), which he eventually chaired.

"Pretty soon I was categorized as the most militant Indian in Nebraska," he recalled during the interview for this book in 1989. But in what he called a "180-degree turn," he later served on the American Indian Policy Review Commission, as president of the National Congress of American Indians, and as tribal chairman of the ten thousand-member Winnebago nation for ten years. A deeply religious person, Snake, who died in 1993, was active in the Native American church, which is known for the use of peyote, a hallucinogen derived from cactus, in its rituals.

Nebraska Congressman Doug Bereuter, whose district includes the Winnebago Reservation, saw him as a bridge builder to the non-Indian community—"a trusted and admired national figure among Indians, with a demonstrated capacity for leadership."

•　•　•

To the truckers traveling U. S. 75 through the hilly Nebraska countryside from Sioux City to Omaha, the Black Hawk Community Center in Winnebago, Nebraska, probably seems just another one-story street-front building in yet another struggling rural community.

To Reuben Snake, however, it's home—the focus of activity here on the Winnebago Indian Reservation, the center of his own earlier work as chief of the Winnebago Tribe, and a place from which to look outward from an Indian perspective on the values and ethics of the rest of the world.

What he sees both troubles and encourages him.

"By and large, the traditional [Indian] teachings are not occurring at a level at which they need to occur," he says during an interview here at the one-room office of the tribe's weekly newspaper. "Most of our children are bombarded by the media—they get their messages from the television." As a result, he explains, "it's real hard to be an Indian in this present day—a real spiritual person, the way that we're taught to be."

The challenge, for Snake, arises because of "this great struggle between the technologically oriented thinkers and the intuitive thinkers. There are a lot of us intuitive thinkers left, but at times I get the feeling that we're fighting a losing battle—because as each generation gets sucked into the use of technology, they get lazy."

In his view, the indigenous American peoples were not lazy, either physically or mentally. "When you think about people living for forty thousand years here, surviving as long as they did and creating the kind of civilizations that we had here—the classic examples being the Mayan and the Incan civilizations—there was a lot of good, solid thinking that went on."

Now, he worries that "European people," preaching the dominance of technology, are eroding the native patterns of thinking. "What does it add to the quality of life to have a TV in every room, and drive four cars, and fly across the continent in three hours? It doesn't make me a better human being to be in contact with all of that."

What spawned that technological thinking? Snake, whose first and last names reflect the mixture of Christian and Indian traditions in which he was raised, lays the blame on a literal interpretation of the Biblical teaching that God gave man dominion over the earth. That idea, says Snake, has led people to think that "they can control nature" through technology—a concept that has given them "a false sense of superiority."

By contrast, he says, "the Indian is a part of the creation, and we're supposed to fit into and be harmonious with the creation—to live in harmony with all that's going on, and not to have the thought that we can dominate any part of it."

Looking at the challenges facing America and the world, Snake sees the need for "a major attitudinal shift" in values. What values would he put forward from his own culture? In answer, he recalls the ethical education he received from his grandfather, who taught him that there were "three things that made the enjoyment of human life possible—three things that people were supposed to exhibit in their everyday activities."

• *Respect.* "The first one is respect for your fellow man. Each one of us is endowed by the Creator with His spirit. The spirit that makes you stand up and walk and talk and see and hear and think is the same spirit that exists in me—there's no difference. So when you look at me, you're looking at yourself—and I'm seeing me in you.

"And the rest of the creation is likewise—the rocks, the trees, everything has the power of the Creator within it. You have to respect that, and try your best not to harm the rest of the creation."

• *Compassion.* "When you look at all the other parts of creation, all the other living creatures—the Creator endowed them with gifts that are far better than ours," says Snake. "There's no human being anywhere near as powerful as a grizzly bear. The eagle flies way up in the sky, and he can see a little mouse going through the grass—and you and I can't see that way. We don't have the fleetness of the deer—you can't catch a deer in a footrace. And the otter: when something is coming from a distance, that otter is the first one to hear. He'll sit up and listen, and he knows what's going on before any of the other creatures know it.

"So as my grandfather was saying, we're pitiful human beings. We don't have any of those physical attributes that the Creator put into everything else. For that reason, we have to be compassionate with one another and help one another—to hold each other up, support one another down the road of life."

• *Honor.* "It's real easy to point fingers at one another for our shortcomings," Snake recalls his grandfather saying.

"But to show somebody the feelings of pride that you have in them for what they do that's beneficial to their fellow man—to stand them up and to put something beautiful on them, a robe or a blanket or a necklace, some beautiful object, and to gather food up and feed all the people and say, 'I want to feed you and break bread with you because of this person'—that takes effort. But if you go to that kind of effort, then you're going to have that good feeling that we have to have one for another. And that's what makes life enjoyable."

Snake also notes that Indians share some of the key Biblical teachings concerning killing, stealing, and sexual morality, although they see them in slightly different ways.

"The Ten Commandments—'Thou shalt not kill,' 'Thou shalt not steal'—to my way of thinking, I don't know of any particular group of people that really abided by those," he says. He notes that even the United States, which he thinks of as "a Christian nation," supplies arms that fuel wars around the world.

He acknowledges that Indian communities are not free of warlike thinking. "Probably the most serious shortcoming of tribal governments is their inability to effectively resolve conflict within the tribe and externally," he says. Here again, however, he feels that the problem arises in part from a loss of traditions.

In earlier times, he says, "if there were a person who received some injury from some person outside [of the Winnebago tribe], and he wanted to avenge that hurt, he [prepared for] a war journey." Before setting out, however, he would have to explain the situation to the tribal elders, who would try to dissuade him from going. If that proved impossible, the elders would appoint someone to follow the war party and, when they stopped for the night, to lay down his pipe in front of the group's leader. "If he picked up this pipe and smoked it with him, then everything was going to be OK, and they would go back to the village, and that would be it," says Snake. "But if he stepped over that pipe, then the tribe had no further commitment to that individual."

That ritual, says Snake, was repeated twice. "They gave him two opportunities to think about it and change his mind. If he didn't, he knew that he didn't have the support of the tribe and the community, that he was doing this on his own."

And that, says Snake, was an important decision, given the importance of a sense of community to the Indian. "A tribal person's mentality is different from that of a nontribal person," he explains. "In a nontribal environment, the well-being of the individual is predominant. But in a tribal society, the welfare and well-being of the individual is on a par with the welfare and well-being of the group. As a Winnebago Indian, I first of all think, of any of my actions, 'How is that going to reflect on my people?' "

A second point from the Judeo-Christian tradition—stealing—also figures strongly in the Indian code. Traditionally, says Snake, "stealing was unthought of. The Indian lived in a lodge, and couldn't put a padlock on the door. Children were taught that what is in that person's lodge is theirs, and you're not supposed to touch it. When the person leaves his lodge, he lays a log down across the doorway. That means there's no one home, so don't come in. Everybody respected that.

"So from the earliest beginnings of a person's childhood, they were taught that if there's something you want, you have to learn how to make it. If you want a buckskin shirt, or moccasins, or if you want a bow, or if you want some kind of instrument or tool, you have to acquire that knowledge. And there were people who could help you acquire that knowledge, so that you could gain the skills of survival.

"The concept of stealing didn't enter into the game until other people brought that thinking over here," says Snake, "and then it became part of the plains culture." Although Winnebagos were "canoe people from the Great Lakes" rather than horse people, the horse became the status symbol for tribes on the plains. As a result, "stealing each other's horses became a part of the culture," he says.

Related to the prohibitions against stealing and the requirements to make whatever you need, Snake explains, are the codes governing the relations between the sexes. "People were taught not to seek marriage until they were capable of going out and getting their food, building their own lodge, and making their own clothing—both male and female. When they were recognized by their elders as being capable of doing these things, then a person could go over there to this lodge and give them all the things he had made, and say, 'This is a gift from me, because I think very highly of your daughter and I'd like her to be my mate, and this is my token of respect to you.' And in return, these people would gather all the things that she was capable of doing and bring that over to his family, and say, 'We think that because your son showed us that he's capable of doing all these things, he's able to take care of our daughter, so we're going to let her become his mate.' "

The result would be a marriage that, traditionally, was expected to last. The elders, says Snake, "taught us that we should be like the eagles when we mate—we should mate for life, because eagles come together and they never part." He worries, however, that divorce has become "so acceptable in our society" that it threatens the very concept of the family, which he regards as "the root of every social order."

Central to the strength of the family are the attitudes toward women. A male child, Snake explains, is traditionally "left under the care and keeping of his female relatives for the first four years of his life, so that he's going to learn the importance of womankind in the society. As he grows up, he's going to have respect for womankind—he's not going to abuse her, and therefore when the time comes that he's going to have a mate of his own, he's going to treat that person with the same regard that he does his grandmother and his mother and his aunt."

What, finally, does Snake see as the need for the future?

"Well, you guys all need to go back to Europe," he says with a laugh.

Then, turning serious, he notes that "our ethics, our moral principles, come out of our spiritual and religious training. So whatever spiritual way we practice, it has moral standards that it teaches us, and we're supposed to live by those. But how many of us do live by the moral, religious principles we were taught in our childhood?"

Snake sees "a dichotomy in our land and in our world. There are people who are concerned about people, and there are people who are concerned about things." He is encouraged, however, by the fact that the numbers of those who are "thinking about people and each other" is "beginning to grow."

"Everybody—I don't care what color, creed, ethnic origin their roots are—we're all the same. We all have common roots. In spite of all of these technological achievements, we're beginning to understand that there is a oneness to the whole universe—there is a oneness."

James A. Joseph

Ethics and 'the L word, Love'

*I knew of no one in government who would sit
back and ask, 'Is this the loving thing to do?'*

One day in 1963, James A. Joseph sat in a car
in downtown Tuscaloosa, Alabama, waiting for
a friend who was visiting a travel agent. The
Louisiana-born and Yale-educated Joseph, an ordained
minister of Afro-American descent, had recently come to
town to teach at all-black Stillman College. There, he had
quickly taken a leadership role in the civil rights movement.
Although protests were already raging in nearby Selma and

Birmingham, Tuscaloosa had been quiet—largely, Joseph recalls, for fear of the Ku Klux Klan, whose state headquarters was there.

That day, unknown to Joseph, the Klan was holding a meeting in the building housing the travel bureau. "Word got around that I was outside," he says, "and they surrounded my car and started shaking it and threatening me. I thought it was the end—because, unlike a mass meeting where you work yourself up into a psychological state that you could take on the world without fear, I was caught off guard." Paralyzed with fright, it took him ten minutes to collect his wits enough to start the car and simply drive through the crowd.

It was a lesson in mental preparedness that later stood him in good stead when, as leader of numerous protest marches, he was attacked by state troopers with billy clubs and cattle prods, by Klansmen with baseball bats, and by townspeople after a black church was tear-gassed. "They called me regularly every night," he says of the Klansmen, "threatening to kill my [infant] son."

In the years since, Joseph has served as head of the Cummins Engine Foundation and as undersecretary of the Department of the Interior in the Carter administration. Now, as president of the Washington-based Council on Foundations, he heads an umbrella organization for more than one thousand American philanthropies.

Robert Rankin, who was chaplain at the Claremont Colleges in Claremont, California, before Joseph succeeded to that position in the 1960s, attributes Joseph's success to his ability to combine a "passion for social justice" with an equally strong "passion for personal religious fulfillment. These things are often quite separate in the white community," notes Rev. Rankin. "With Jim you saw these two polarities become one."

•   •   •

Part way into a conversation on global values in his downtown Washington office, James Joseph brings up one of the central elements in his ethical code. "The *L* word," he calls it. "Love."

These days, he laments, "nobody talks about it any more. I think there is as much shyness away from the *L* word *love* as there has been from the *L* word *liberal*. Ethicists used to say that that's what ethics is about: when you asked, 'Ought I to do this?' you asked, 'Is it the loving thing to do?' I think that's still a helpful way to think about what is right and what is good."

The problem, he acknowledges, is that "the word *love* is used in so many ways." For him, the real meaning of the word hardly resides in the "mushy kind of thing" that many imagine it to be. When you talk about love as part of an ethical code, he says, "you're not talking about what [American rock star] Madonna is talking about." The real meaning, he insists, is closer to the idea of loving your enemy that was so central to the civil rights movement.

"It's respecting the humanity of the individual—not because of who they are, but *in spite of* what they might be," he says. "It's difficult to talk about loving [Iraqi president] Saddam Hussein, you know, but that's what the Christian concept means. It doesn't mean *liking* Saddam. But since we've confused loving with liking, it's difficult to use the word."

Also high on his list for a code of ethics are three words that, he admits, are "so interrelated it's difficult to separate them": respect, tolerance, and fairness.

"When I think about the challenges of the nineties and the next century," he says, "I probably would begin with respect for others." By that, he means "respect for the uniqueness of the individual, respect for the cultures of other communities, respect for the need to begin to integrate into our collective memory appreciation for the contributions and traditions of those who are different."

One of the fundamental difficulties of the present age, he says, is the "polarization and fragmentation and Balkanization" that arises when the traditions of others are not respected. "It is very difficult for people to think in terms of membership in a larger community unless there is a sense of respect for the smaller community of which they are part. That is why the more interdependent we become as a society, the more people are turning to smaller communities of meaning and belonging."

For Joseph, "the search for common grounds begins with the search for beginnings. Until there is respect for the uniqueness of the individual and his or her community, I don't think you'll get those individuals thinking in terms of membership in the larger community. I think the missing element is respect."

That lack of respect, he feels, is becoming more evident as the century advances. It leads, he says, to the growing fragmentation of society, apparent not only in an upsurge of racism in America but in the practice of "ethnic cleansing" in the former Yugoslavia and in what he calls "tribalism in the former Soviet Union." He worries that earlier efforts in these nations to create communities out of disparate groups are "unraveling" into divisiveness.

"We're going back to where we were before we formed those larger communities," he says. "I think that unless we develop respect for the uniqueness of all of our traditions, we won't have a basis for common ground. That search for common ground is a fundamental search, and it's going to be an important search in the twenty-first century."

Following naturally from respect, he says, is tolerance. "If you recognize the uniqueness of others, and develop respect for that, then you've got to tolerate." The result, he says, will be "a new kind of pluralism" that is not hierarchical—in which one set of values or one lifestyle is dominant over another—but "an egalitarian pluralism in which we differ but meet on the plane of equality."

And out of tolerance, he says, grows his next point: fairness. "Here one could get caught up in the very complicated theories of social justice," he warns. "Or one could simply look at the Golden Rule. I relate fairness to treating other people as I would want to be treated. I think that [rule] serves humanity well. It ought to be a part of any ethic for the future."

Those four things, he says, "would be fundamental to any kind of ethic I would develop."

Does it matter that this ethic be seen as universal?

"I think it's critically important that there be a global

code of ethics," he asserts, "if we're going to have some form of global community rather than the fragmentation now taking place." The need, however, is not to define this global code in an academic or theoretical way, but to make it practical and effective. "Unless that ethic can somehow bring us together, then it doesn't have any real utility—it remains an abstraction. I think the primary ethical challenge is to bring us together."

To do that, he says, "we have to begin where people are." That's very different, he explains, from "beginning with the ideal," which is typically the way religious institutions approach the question of ethics. "We are accustomed in our religious gatherings to affirming ideals and hoping that they will catch hold." The problem, however, is that "people are not responding."

"You have to begin with where they are and move to the general precepts," he says. In the future, discussions of ethics will have to deal with "ethics and the economy, ethics and justice, ethics and community." That may result, he admits, in "some fragmentation of the discussion of ethics," since "you can't just discuss ethics as ethics, [but only] in relation to something that people identify with."

"The problem with the theological ethicists in the seminary is that they are much too concerned with what Aristotle said in his book of ethics," says Joseph. "That's fine, but a person who doesn't have a job—and who wants to know why it is that I don't have a job even though I'm trying like hell—wants to deal with ethics as it relates to fairness, not as it relates to Aristotle's precepts."

Also interfering with a proper sense of ethics, says Joseph, is the confusion over ethics on one hand and rules on the other. That confusion shows up most prominently, he says, in government, where "ethics means written rules, rather than individual behavior or institutional behavior." When government officials talk about ethics, he says, they usually mean, " 'Have you violated our rule, our policy?' " During his years in the Carter administration, he recalls, "I knew of no one in government who would sit back and ask, 'Is this the loving thing to do?' "

That's not to say that rules are unimportant. Laying out clear definitions of ethical standards often prevents ethical abuses. Case in point: bribery, which so often appears on the horizon of international relations, both in business and in government. "When is it a bribe and when isn't it?" asks Joseph. "That's one of the difficult ethical questions." Here, he notes, a definition helps: "It's probably a bribe if it's to gain a competitive advantage in a secretive way."

Essentially, however, ethics is not a matter of adhering to definitions. Instead, he says, "ethics is about choices: how do you choose the good among competing claims?" It would seem, then, that "ethics would be fundamental" for those who work in government. "But unfortunately, when they talk about ethics, they don't talk about those choices, they talk about rules."

Still another impediment to a clear sense of ethics is what Joseph calls "the preoccupation in the last several years with the microethics of individual behavior to the exclusion of the macroethics of institutional behavior." That preoccupation with microethics, he says, has also shaped politics. In recent years, he notes, "we've been obsessed with how politicians

41

behave toward their partners, whether it's male-male or male-female. We haven't been as concerned about what it means to form a benevolent community, or a benevolent government, or benevolent institutions. If you talk to the average American, they'll say that we've been very concerned with ethics. But we've been concerned with who Bill Clinton had a relationship with, or Gary Hart, or whoever, as opposed to how he used his influence and his power in institutions in which he operated to serve the public good."

But can one distinguish between the personal and the public ethics, or are they one and the same?

"The *personal* grows out of a value commitment," says Joseph, while "the *public* may be a pragmatic more than a personal commitment. The truth is that when I elect a person, I'm concerned that he behave ethically." Whether he does so "because he thinks that's the way he'll get re-elected, or because of his personal commitment, is not that important to me. The point is that he *behave* ethically."

There is, however, a strong requirement that the behavior not be damaging either in public or in private. Returning to the example of President Clinton's alleged marital infidelity—an issue that arose strongly during the campaign in 1992—Joseph notes that "the moment it was clear to me that Hillary Clinton was comfortable with her relationship with Bill Clinton, then I said, 'Who am I to be preoccupied with his behavior?' If Hillary had said, 'He's been a bastard, doing all these extramarital things that are destroying our family!' then I would be very concerned about whether I'd want to give him any power or influence. The moment she says, 'I'm comfortable,' then it doesn't matter to me. The point I'm concerned about is, will he be a good president?"

By analogy, Joseph recalls his own work in the private sector with multinational corporations developing codes of conduct. The first question he asked of any corporate action, he says, was whether it was in obedience to the law. "The second thing was, 'Will somebody be hurt?' The avoidance of social injury becomes a primary ethical imperative. If somebody is doing something that hurts somebody else privately, then I'm very concerned."

So if Hillary Clinton "had indicated that the family was hurt, then I'd have been concerned. Now the question is, Was [her husband] involved in a relationship with somebody else who was hurt? I don't know."

For Joseph, this "microethics" issue concerning the president is part of a broader context: the growing debate in the United States about so-called "family values." Joseph recognizes that the moral values practiced by national leaders do in fact send "signals" to a society "in desperate need of values." But the term "family values," he says, has become little more than a "political football, which means 'other families' values are bad, but my family's values are good.' It's always those other people's values we mean by 'family values.' "

As an example, Joseph recalls watching the news of the riots in south-central Los Angeles in the spring of 1992. The image portrayed, he says, was of "an absence of a value system" in the Afro-American community. In fact, he says, many of the young Afro-Americans involved in the looting and rioting were products of "very religious families" who "hear all sorts of thing about values."

Such families, he says, tend to be "rather conservative about values," although, since they identify strongly with efforts to achieve social justice, they are often classed as liberal. Joseph himself comes from a family where his father "identified with things that even the religious right wouldn't identify with at this point," including prohibitions against dancing and playing cards. "He had a whole spectrum of very conservative values," Joseph recalls.

But if those conservative values are part of the fabric of the Los Angeles Afro-American community, why the riots?

"I think in a moment of rage, one's response transcends those kinds of holds on the personality. So the question is, how do the value commitments that are pervasive in the community become so much a part of individuals that everything they do is based on them?"

The answer? "It's back to community," says Joseph. "How do you build community? How do you build cohesion among disparate elements? Values is one of these. But unless you're willing to admit that one of the values that has primacy in the hierarchy of values is diversity, then you can't engage in the right kind of discussion. Once you are willing to admit that, then you can move to the next level of discussion and ask, 'What are the values that we share in common?' "

One of the common values, he says, must be a "commitment to civil society" by all the diverse groups making up the community. There must also be a commitment to "the use of that intermediate space between the individual and government" that the concept of a civil society affords. "I think there's so much more in common among these groups than we tend to think," he says.

Of critical importance to creating the sense of community, he insists, is education. And central to education is the teaching of ethics. "I think, yes, we've got to teach it," he says.

The problem, he says, is how to present ethics in such a way that the teaching is not "captive to a parochial tradition—so that somebody who's not a part of that tradition is not offended. That's the $64,000 question. I have real problems with those people who say, 'You've got to teach Christian ethics.' Obviously the [American] culture is pervasively Christian in many ways, so you can't teach ethics without that exposure to Christian ethics. But you can't just say to that Jewish kid or that Muslim kid, 'This is all of ethics.' "

"I think you have to start with little things like honesty, and fairness, and tolerance, and respect, with the youngest kids. But you have to deal with them where they are, rather than in some large abstraction."

But if no single religious tradition can provide the ethical teaching, then where will the ethics we teach come from?

It will come, says Joseph, from what he calls "universal norms that are shared in common," such as the four elements of love, respect, tolerance, and fairness he identified as part of his ethical code for the future. "Those are affirmed by all religions," he says.

Another, drawn from his own profession, is "philanthropy or charity." Westerners, he says, "tend to think that it's unique to Europeans. But it's one of the seven pillars of Islam." The idea of caring for one's neighbor, he adds, is "fundamental" to almost all religions. "So if we teach it as a universal norm, then people will come to realize that it's not only important as a value which relates to their prophet or their notion of God. They will also recognize and enlighten their self-interest to take care of the needs of each other."

"The purpose of the schools is to start them thinking ethically and wanting to be ethical. As they develop a desire to know more about a particular tradition of which they've been a part, then they will continue that search themselves."

But can these two ethical imperatives—for diversity and tolerance on one hand and for the continuing search for religious roots on the other—coexist in our society? Answering with an example, Joseph recalls a recent occasion where, as he sat down to lunch with the staff of one of his departments, he was asked to say grace. "That's very unusual," he chuckles, observing that typically "nobody asks." An ordained Christian minister, he agreed, and then, looking across the table, he saw two Jews and a woman from Pakistan among the rest.

On such occasions, he says, most people would probably recall "whatever his parents taught him in the way of a blessing and spout that out." Instead, he tried to think how he could "say something meaningful to each of these people and try to bless this food."

"I think ethics is going to have to be sort of like that," he concludes. "You've got all these people sitting at the table. And unless they recognize in what I am trying to communicate something that relates to them and their tradition, they'll tune me out. So we have to find some way of including everybody at the table, making sure they understand that we are in touch with what gives meaning to them."

Shojun Bando

The Ethics of Love

*It shouldn't be that others should tell you
to love others: it should just come of its
own will, spontaneously.*

Like many Japanese of his generation, Shojun Bando
harbors defining memories of World War II. As a
young child living in the Bando Hoonji Temple, where
his father was the head monk, he remembers watching from
the window of his nearby school as a devastating fire, caused
by the American bombardment, raced across his part of
Tokyo. It broke through the walled-in temple grounds and
licked up several outbuildings—and then miraculously died

before reaching the spacious, ornately carved wooden temple.

Despite such intimations of a supreme harmony, the young Bando spent several years in rebellion against his father's Buddhist religion. "From the age of about sixteen to twenty, I hated to live here," he says with a smile, gesturing around at the temple in which he is now the head priest. "All I could think of was trying to get away."

While enrolled at the University of Tokyo, however, he met two young laymen of the Jodoshin denomination, to which his temple belongs. They encouraged him to spend a summer studying at a nearby temple. "After I came back, I had my mind set that I would replace my father," he says. "That was when I was twenty years old."

Emerging from the university in 1957 with a master of arts degree, Bando studied at Oxford for a year before taking up academic positions at Otani University in Kyoto and Ueno Gakuen College in Tokyo. The author of several books, including *Chi to Ai no Katachi* [Expressions of Wisdom and Compassion], he has been a visiting professor at the University of Hawaii and a lecturer at Oberlin College in the United States.

Now, as the twenty-seventh monk in a line of succession that dates from the founding of his temple in 1214, he preaches to a growing congregation that gathers weekly on the straw tatami mats spread out before the intricate gold-leafed altar and the statue of Buddha. He is also a frequent commentator on religious issues for NHK, the state-run broadcasting company. "He exudes a deep reverence for people, for life, for ideas, even for little things" says Carl

Becker, a professor of comparative religion at Kyoto University and one of only a handful of non-Japanese ever to receive an appointment in the Japanese civil service. "Those who know him call him 'Bosatsu'—*saint* or *enlightened sage*—behind his back."

Bando, a scholarly and hospitable man who once studied under the Japanese Zen scholar D. T. Suzuki, notes that although the temple building has "become dilapidated" in the decades since it was constructed in the 1930s, he resists refurbishing it. When people come to the temple, he says, "their motives are not so much that they want to listen to difficult sermons, but that they seek tranquillity and serenity of atmosphere." Old buildings like this, he says, "give you peace of mind. They shouldn't be torn down."

During a two-hour interview over green tea served by his wife at a low table surrounded by cushions, Bando spoke in Japanese. The translation is by Hiroko Sakata, a professional interpreter.

●　●　●

For Shojun Bando, the ethics of the next century must flow from a single reigning concept: love.

"Each person thinks that he is the most important person in the world," says Bando. "It's true for everyone. So the more you think you are the most important, the more naturally it has to flow back to the fact that so are the others. It shouldn't be that *others* should tell you to love others: it should just come of its own will, spontaneously."

This idea, he says, is "the basic foundation on which the ethics of Buddhism lies."

What does he mean by the word *love?* The Japanese word, he explains, is *jihi*, which means compassion toward others. "The meaning of *jihi* is to accept the sadness of others as being the sadness of yourself," he says. Tracing his ideas to a concept laid down by the Indian philosopher Nâgârjuna—the so-called "Augustine and Aquinas" of Buddhism, often seen as second in importance only to Buddha in Buddhist history—Bando divides *jihi* into three stages.

In the first, or humanistic, stage, love is largely intertwined with egotism. An individual example of such love, he says, is "someone who has a lot of assets, and just because he wants to show off he gives them to a nonprofit organization."

"That would be good in a social sense," he says, "but it's also trying to satisfy your ego."

The second stage he describes as "conditional love." It still involves some sense of egoism, since the depth of the love "depends on whether you like the person or dislike the person. This is conditional love, because you're influenced by your feeling, the emotion you have toward that person."

In the third stage, which he calls "unconditional love," the egoism disappears. "You don't question the kind of person to be loved—it's unconditional, you love that person no matter what."

According to Nâgârjuna, only the third kind of love can "really benefit the world," says Bando. If love rises only to the other two stages, "instead of benefiting the world, it will have adverse effects on the world." The problem today is that "people around the world think the number one and number two *jihi* are true compassion."

Where does he place his own culture on that scale? "Unfortunately," he says, "Japan is still at the number one or number two stage." He adds, however, that the sense of compassion "is deepening, in a good way. Because people see the adverse effects of industrialization—the pollution they hear about on the media—they tend to look for solutions. I think people are now more sensitized to the needs. They are more aware."

That sense of adversity, he says, is often required in order to move societies forward toward the third stage of love. "It often happens that people, unless they're up against difficulties, their eyes will not open up."

In order for this highest sense of love to develop, there must be a clear understanding of what Bando calls "the relation between individuals and society." In order for the individual to "stand on his own feet, he has to get support from society. But if an individual asserts his opinion too much, then he is going to clash with other people." To strike the proper balance here requires a quality that Bando places high on his code of values: wisdom.

"In Buddhism," he explains, "it is often taught that true wisdom makes a true individual." The effect of wisdom, he explains, is to "achieve detachment—nonattachment—and to get away from being immersed in too many *things*." This kind of wisdom, he says, is central to achieving the third stage of love, since "real giving cannot be realized until you can be completely detached from the idea that 'I am giving you something—this particular thing to that

person.' Wisdom is the function of attaining this detachment, getting away from being too attached to things."

Does the highest sense of love and wisdom, then, lead
to the conclusion that the material world is unreal?

For Bando, reality comprises "things that appear one
after another as time passes, as things are changing." In
Buddhism, he explains, the material world is "there only
temporarily. It's not an entity or substance. We don't call
it void. We don't call it empty. But we don't call it substance.
It's there for the time being."

Would a Buddhist, then, engage in social action in the
face of a material world apparently full of great evil and
injustice, even though that action might create a certain
amount of disharmony and disturb one's own sense of detachment?

"This is very difficult," Bando admits. "I think that I
would really come and say something in the open, but
whether or not I would take actual action—it depends on
the situation. I think that through people with whom I have
connections, I would keep on saying to society, 'This is
wrong.' It needs to be said repeatedly."

Reflecting on his experience growing up during World
War II, he recalls that another one of his strongly held precepts—that you must not kill—seemed threatened by the
military training that at that time extended down into junior
high school. The students who were one year ahead of him,
he recalls, "were already training with live ammunition how
to shoot people. If the war had gone on one more year, I
would have gone to training with live ammunition."

Now, if ordered by his government to shoot someone,

he has no question about his answer. "I would refuse," he says. "I would say, 'I cannot do this.' "

So the ideal of individual freedom is very important, even though it may lead to conflicts with society?

"Yes, of course," he says. "The question is one of judgment. You have to reflect on the universal precept, the universal principle, and determine whether your judgment is right or wrong." That requires turning back "to the original teaching of the saints" to locate the principles and test individual decisions.

"All we can do is to listen to the traditional teachings, which include universal truth, universal precepts," he says. "People lending their ears and people abiding by that—it's all we can do."

Another precept on Bando's code is equality. His sense of equality begins by "admitting that each person is different, that each person has his own individuality." That, he says, is very different from "treating people exactly the same"—a point he illustrates in relation to the growing tension in his own country over the role of women in society.

"Women have different characteristics from men right from the moment they are born," he observes, "and you cannot look at them as being completely the same as men. It is important that the individual differences between women and men be emphasized. That is equality: individual differences emphasized as human beings."

At the moment, he says, there is a "fervent debate" under way within Buddhist circles about the propriety of allowing women to become monks. His own views on the matter are shaped largely by his particular history: the temple

a strong role in ethical instruction if given the freedom
to do so.

• *Television.* It is clear to Bando that a sense of ethics develops in quiet reflection rather than in noisy activity—a fact that leads him to "feel strongly, in my bones" that television is highly detrimental to modern society.

"The mind that is able to do meditation, to think deeply, is being perturbed by television," he says. "This is a serious problem indeed."

He is encouraged, however, by recent studies showing that middle-aged and elderly Japanese "have gotten away from looking at television so much" and "are now listening more to the radio." One sign: an hour-long religious program airing on radio daily at 4 A.M. is rapidly increasing its audience—"so much so," he says, "that the people who plan this program are surprised." Each week, he says, it covers a variety of topics from the perspective of Buddhism, Christianity, Shintoism, and the so-called "new religions" as well.

How does he explain this newfound interest in religion? "I think that because of this increasing noise—the television is turned on in the home day in and day out—people are getting tired of all this and are turning away and coming more to religion."

For Bando, that should naturally mean an improvement in the moral condition of society, which he sees as one of humanity's most vital measures. That importance, he says, became clear to him in the aftermath of the war.

"The military sector used to say, 'We're winning the

war! We're on our way to victory!' " he says. "They would even lie in their propaganda."

In the face of that propaganda, however, Bando recalls that his mentor D. T. Suzuki predicted the defeat of Japan because, in his view, the Japanese military had no moral basis and therefore could not possibly succeed. "It did not take such a long time before everything came to an end, and it turned out that the Japanese *had* lost—and that they had tricked, or betrayed, the Japanese public all along."

For all of his nation's present and past problems, however, Bando remains optimistic that the ethical barometer will rise. "When people are in a state of abundancy and they're rich and satisfied," he says, commenting on what he sees as the situation of Japan until very recently, "the religious aspect is asleep within them."

"The more difficulties there are around you," he concludes, "the more religious people get."

Le Ly Hayslip

Helping Each Other Grow

*What am I doing here? I'm here to serve
mankind—it doesn't matter what I 'do.'*

U ntil the age of twelve, Le Ly Hayslip grew up like
most children in rural Vietnam—learning to survive
by planting rice, harvesting coconuts, raising pigs
and chickens, tending water buffalo, cooking on a three-
brick stove, forecasting next year's weather from studying
beehives and anthills, and living within the centuries-old
order of her close-knit Buddhist family, where she was the
youngest of six children.

All that changed when, in 1965, 3,500 U.S. troops landed in her small village of Ky La, near Da Nang, at the start of one the bitterest and most ambiguous wars of this century. Survival now meant crawling, hiding, and eating whatever was available. It also meant being forced to serve whichever army was closest at hand as spy and saboteur. By sixteen, Phung Thi Le Ly (her Vietnamese name) had been raped by the Viet Cong and tortured by the South Vietnamese. She had suffered the deaths of several of her family members, fled to Da Nang, and worked as a domestic servant for a Vietnamese family. And she had given birth to a son fathered by her wealthy employer.

After working in the wartime black market, she returned to her village in 1968—by then mostly leveled by the Americans—where her father, severely beaten by the Viet Cong, urged her to devote herself not to war, vengeance, or profiteering, but to her son, Jimmy. Within days of that visit, her father killed himself. "I was no longer confused with where my duty lay," she writes in her autobiography, *When Heaven and Earth Changed Places: A Vietnamese Woman's Journey From War to Peace*, published in 1989. "With the Viet Cong? With the legal government and its allies? With the peasants in the countryside? No—my duty lay with my son, and with nurturing life, period."

In 1969 she married an American civilian contractor from San Diego, Ed Munro, and began another wrenching transition, this time to suburban living in southern California, where her second son, Tommy, was born. After Munro died in 1973, she married Dennis Hayslip, a computer operator for the U. S. Customs Service, who went to Vietnam in 1975 and arranged to get Le Ly's sister, Lan, and her two children out of the country the day before the communists took over. Le Ly's youngest son, Alan, was born that year; Hayslip himself died in an automobile accident in 1982.

In 1985, before Jimmy left for college, she and her son finally began writing a book describing the war from the perspective of the Vietnamese people. The next year, after opening a Chinese-Vietnamese restaurant and completing several successful real estate transactions, she returned to Vietnam, rebuilt her relations with her family, and began working on the joint projects that would ultimately lead her to found, in 1989, the East Meets West Foundation, which she still heads. Beginning as a vehicle to construct and operate a rural medical clinic in her native village, this nonprofit peace and relief organization is now building the Peace Village Rehabilitation Center in China Beach, where the U. S. forces launched their first military offensive of the war. The center opened its medical facility in 1991.

Hayslip's first book, now the subject of a movie by Hollywood director Oliver Stone, was followed in 1993 by her second, *Child of War, Woman of Peace*. She lives in a modest house outside of San Diego, California, which she shares with her sons and with the crowded offices of her foundation.

● ● ●

Le Ly Hayslip is a survivor: that much is clear from her biography. But it is only midway through an hour-long interview in her hillside Escondido home that this petite, lively woman finally articulates the mental stance that has ensured her survival.

"We cannot grow unless we learn something," she says in clear but heavily accented English. "And every obstacle in front of us, every second, is for us to learn so we can grow."

For Hayslip, those two ideas—learning and growing, often through suffering but always with compassion for others—lay the foundation for all that humanity can accomplish. As she talks about the need for a global set of values, these two ideas shape themselves into three questions that, she says, every individual around the world needs to ask: "where is he coming from, why is he here, and what is he here for?"

The first question finds answers in the Buddhist cosmology of Hayslip's upbringing. "He comes from wind, fire, water, and dust," she explains, adding that "you live in this planet, you must have spring, winter, fall, and summer. Then you have east, north, south, and west. All this is twelve elements."

Out of these elements, she says, four races arise—red, yellow, white, and black. However different they seem to be, "you cannot separate" one from the other, since humanity "comes together as a package." Just as you cannot destroy fire—even though you can use water to put it out for the moment—so you cannot destroy any of the other aspects of humanity and the universe.

"You cannot say, 'I go to north, but I'm never going to south.' You can't."

Reflecting the Buddhist concept of reincarnation, she traces her own lineage from "the lowest fish and worm" to her present form. "I've been here 8,780,000 lifetimes," she says in a matter-of-fact tone, noting that every lifetime has added to her progress and growth and helped her understand where she comes from.

She answers the second question—"why is he here?" —with equal directness. "He is here for growth. The basis is growing." Just as a planted tree or a young child will grow, so the individual on "the spiritual level" must understand that he or she is "spiritually growing."

Of the "seven planets on the map of the world," she says, "this is the lowest planet there is. This is the elementary school." It is on this planet, she explains, that God has put us to "learn to become a human being. God makes everything happen."

Then who is God? "In the east," she says, "we call Him Mr. Sky. Anywhere you look out there—now it's gray, sometimes it's dark, sometimes it's blue—that is where God is. We refer to Him like a personal friend—not like a Westerner, [for whom] God is a person only good for the Christian use. No. We relate to Him because we [all are part] of Him. He makes us."

The purpose of this earthly experience, then, is to become the best human being we can be—a point emphasized by Buddha. "Buddha is a teacher, who said, 'Look, in this society you have to be calm, you have to be compassionate, you have to love one another, you have to understand the basis of why you're here.' When the people misunderstand about God and Buddha and all that, it becomes separation, it becomes disconnected. It becomes, 'I'm better than you, or you're better than others.' It's not so. When you're talking about the global getting along or not getting along, we're too much separated. We don't understand the basic need."

Answering her third question—"What are we here for?"—she says simply that, "We're here so that we can help each other to grow." Using a graphic analogy, she notes that "when you step on a needle, you put your two thumbs together and you try to push that needle back out. That is why we need each other—to push, to grow. Without each other, we can't grow. Without Hitler, we can't grow. Without Ho Chi Minh, we can't grow. Without John F. Kennedy, we can't grow. All of those leaders are needed for us to grow. Without war, we can't learn peace. Without peace, we cannot have compassion. All of those things have to work together for us to grow."

Working together, however, does not only involve world leaders and social elites. It embraces everyone, from those who mop the floor to those who are "riding the big truck." The farmer who plants rice, raises ducks, and brings eggs to the market is just as important a "servant" as anyone else. "We need each other in every way, in every function, so that we can grow," she says. "That is why we're here."

Turning these three questions more specifically to herself, Hayslip notes that they can be answered on two different levels. "If you ask me, 'What is my name?' I will say, 'My name is Le Ly Hayslip.' If you ask, 'Where are you coming from?' I'll say, 'I come from Vietnam.' [If you ask],

'What are you doing here now?' I will say, 'I'm a writer and a mother.' "

Answered on a deeper, more "gut level," however, she would say that her name is simply, "I am I—that is the only entity I come with." As for where she comes from, she notes that "I come from God"—a point she feels with particular force, having been born prematurely of a mother who had attempted an abortion. And "what am I doing here? I'm here to serve mankind—it doesn't matter what I 'do.' "

While her sense of serving mankind involves love and compassion, it also includes a fair degree of tolerance. When individuals or groups find they cannot work together as one, "then we [can] all work together differently." If certain groups will not let themselves be helped, she says, then "leave them alone. If we cannot like them, at least learn how to live with them. You have your own job, you eat your own food. How you make that food is up to you, and how I live my life is up to me." Without that sense of tolerance, she says, "we create a big problem for others. Then that problem will come back, and come back, and come back. People don't understand about that, but it's very simple and very basic."

This tolerance and understanding lies at the root of her current work as a bridge builder between two cultures. The reason the two countries she knows so well had to endure such terrible suffering—the one physically and militarily, the other politically and spiritually—is simply so that each could grow. She has seen this growth take place in her own organization, as veterans from the United States have endured "a lot of pain" by returning to Vietnam to do humanitarian work. She has also seen Vietnamese refugees, who were "basically wealthy, high officers, well educated," come to the United States and "overnight become janitors, dishwashers, waiters. Why? For him to grow. Now he can go back and help the country to rebuild."

Her own life, she says, exemplifies her point. "I came over here and learned how to live in a house with a carpet and how to cook with the stove, gas and electric. I learned how to watch TV, which I didn't have before. I learned how to drive a car—which isn't a water buffalo! That is my own growing."

Now, she says, her purpose is to use that growth to "tell people how my life used to be" and to build greater understanding of her culture. The opportunity to do so came when her book fell into the hands of Oliver Stone, whose credits include two previous Oscar-winning movies about Vietnam, *Platoon* and *Born on the Fourth of July*. As an adviser during the filming, Hayslip says she "walked step by step to show Oliver Stone how our life was, how we live in our village, how we eat, and how we take care of our families and our ancestors so that we can teach others."

As she helps build such cultural bridges, she is well aware that some criticize her for abandoning her own heritage and favoring her adopted country. "Some people say I'm never going back to where I was before," she says. The point, she explains, is that "I learn everything here, and take it back to Vietnam to help them to grow." She is not, however, interested in imposing the West's materialism on Vietnam. "No way will I bring them the carpet to put into the house.

No way will I ask them to ride a car rather than a water buffalo. I can do better things. I can build a hospital. I can send the doctor over there to teach."

She also feels that she has a role in teaching Westerners some of the values of the Vietnamese. Foremost among them: survival.

"If war happened to come to the United States, people here could not survive," she says. "There are no survival basics. It doesn't matter how many wars go on in Vietnam, because we can survive. We have survival skills. Over here, you get in a car, you ride to San Diego to buy the groceries, you pick up a hamburger on the way home through the window. What if the whole city is without electricity? Or there's no gas? You can't ride in the car, you can't walk that far. All the basic things—he's not prepared. He's not ready—including me. But at least I know it's coming. It's up to me whether I'm ready or not ready."

It is not only the material surroundings of the West that concern Hayslip, however. She is most troubled by the effect of materialism on the soul. "In Vietnam, if my neighbor's children come and knock on my door and say, 'My mother's going to have a baby,' the whole village comes to help. The first instinct is to save life. Whereas over here, if I'm sick and my children go knock on the door, the only thing my neighbor can do is to call an ambulance. I'll be dead before an ambulance comes here! If you come into my house and see me lying here very sick, you don't dare to move me, because you're not a doctor. So where is your human obligation? Where is your human instinct to try to save me? You don't have it. You lost it, because there are too many rules."

In Vietnam, she says, "if you come into my house and you step on glass and cut your foot, I didn't put the glass there to hurt you—it was an accident. I'll bring you in and try my best to heal you. Over here, the first thing you do is you call your insurance, the next thing is a lawyer. All of this really, really hurts the soul deeply. That's why we're so lonely. That's why we're so empty. You live in a huge house, and you drive a big car, and you have more than you ever wanted. But we don't have a neighbor, a family unit. So how can you be global? Everybody is separated from everybody."

"So I teach the American people from here. I bring them back to Vietnam to show them all the basics for survival. What does the man from the West learn from us? He learns how to survive and be humble." He also learns, she says, to appreciate and to forgive. "The war is over in Vietnam. If everyone in Vietnam can forgive and love us," she says, speaking of herself now as an American, "why can't we do the same?"

At bottom, then, what matters to Hayslip is the quality of an individual's thinking. Asked what would constitute the most perfect person she could imagine, she says unhesitatingly, "You have to have a right thought." It is clear to her that thought determines the nature of the universe. "The whole universe is spinning so fast because of our thoughts. If [we] slow down and go to sleep, the world stops spinning. What are we thinking of? Are we thinking good, bad, or ugly? If everybody thinks good, good things result. If everybody thinks bad, bad things come. If everybody thinks ugly, the whole world becomes uglier. Everybody has to control their own mind and thinking. That's what you call right thoughts. If I'm thinking about war, I'll go out and get the army. If I'm thinking of peace, I'll go out and do some peace work. It is all based on our thinking."

How, then, does humanity bend its efforts toward peace? Hayslip turns to a kind of personal allegory for her answer. "I have three sons named Jimmy, Tommy, and Alan," she says. Jimmy's father is Vietnamese—"yellow skinned," as she puts it. Tommy's father is white. And suppose, she says, that Alan was born in Africa of a black father. Then suppose all the fathers died, and she died as well.

Thirty years later, the three sons become diplomats, each representing their respective countries at the United Nations. "Three of them sit at a round table discussing religion, politics, and human rights. They answer that their country is better, their religion is better. So they fight, they start a war with each other. And I become a beautiful angel and stand right in front of them and say, 'Children, stop fighting. I am your mother, you are brothers. You come from my womb. You are all my children.' You think they believe me? No way!"

"That is what God is about. He tells them that every day, He is in millions of places. He gives all the religion we need to understand Him. But we argue against Him. 'No, I'm yellow, I can't be your child.' 'I'm black, I can't be your child.' 'I'm white, I can't be your child.' "

And while this sort of thinking "makes lots of sense" to us, she concludes that "all of this is nonsense to Him."

Bernard Przewozny

Global Environmentalism and a Life-Liberating Ethic

The earth and its natural goods are the inheritance of all peoples. There is a social obligation to private property.

I t's little wonder that Father Bernard Przewozny looks at the world from a global and interdisciplinary perspective. Born of Polish parents, raised in Canada, educated at St. Hyacinth College and Seminary in Granby, Massachusetts, in the United States, he now resides at the Pontifical Theological Faculty of St. Bonaventure in Rome, where he is a tenured professor of Christology. After studying chemistry and physics in the early sixties, he worked as an engineer in

Canada. Now, with a doctorate in sacred theology, he is a Franciscan of the Order of Friars Minor Conventional.

These many strands have converged, in ways he describes as "inevitable," into an abiding concern for environmental issues that began in the early 1980s. At that time, he became one of the first promoters of the International "Terra Mater" Seminars held in Gubbio, Italy. After working to organize the 25th Anniversary Celebrations of the World Wildlife Fund in Assisi in 1986, he served on a number of study groups sponsored by the Pontifical Academy of Sciences on such topics as agriculture and the quality of life, tropical forests and the conservation of species, and resources and population.

He was one of the Vatican Delegated Observers to the 1990 Seoul Conference on Justice, Peace, and Integrity of Creation, organized by the World Council of Churches. A year earlier, in 1989, he had been instrumental in establishing the Franciscan Center of Environmental Studies in Rome. The center instituted the International Saint Francis Prize for the Environment, which he administers. The author of two books and numerous articles, he is working with the center on the establishment of a botanical garden of trees that possess symbolic value in the world's great religions.

"He really does have the matter of interfaith communication about environmental matters very well in mind and in a very interesting way," says Peter Raven, director of the Missouri Botanical Garden and home secretary of the National Academy of Sciences, who calls him "a really deep thinker about global ethics from a religious perspective."

● ● ●

Bernard Przewozny admits it: he is an unashamed meeting-goer. In recent years, he has attended conferences on the environment in various parts of the world, worked on numerous committee reports, and maintained constant contact with colleagues around the globe.

From that deep immersion one trend stands out: these days, he says, "ethics is being delinked from a global vision."

During a late-afternoon interview at his college in a suburb of Rome, he explains his concern that the global vision so necessary to formulate sound environmental policy for the future is typically based only on "scientific input, political input, technical input." Missing, he says, is a consistent effort to incorporate an ethical viewpoint into such policy.

"That happened in Brussels in 1989," he says, recalling one of many examples. As part of a working group commissioned by the European Community to focus on environmental policy, he found that many of his colleagues wanted to develop their report with no attention to ethical concerns—and then, almost as an afterthought, to "let the religious people give us some sort of ethics" to bolster the conclusions.

"They tried to deduce from a global vision a global ethics," he says. "It is my contention that does not work." Instead, he argues, the ethical issues have to be woven into the thinking from the very start.

The dangers of delinking ethics in this way are illustrated for Father Przewozny by the tale of a dam-building project in Nepal in the late 1970s. The developers, he said, used environmental impact models developed in Austria, "forgetting that the Himalayas are a different system" where terraced farming produces a different pattern of water use. Midway through construction, he says, there was "a tremendous rain storm" that "simply leveled [the dam] before it got into full function."

"It was the best thing that could have happened," he says, because, had it been completed, it would have destroyed traditional ways of farming, despite assurances to the inhabitants that the dam would "work" for them.

A much better model, he says, is to "bring in representatives from different religions and different cultures" at the outset, to help planners understand "the local ethics, the local cultural values" before they establish policy. Such values "have to be strengthened" if a global environmental vision is to succeed.

He is not blind, however, to the difficulties of attending to local values in real-world situations of cultural diversity and conflict. He recalls working on an environmental action plan for the southern Mediterranean, with its many different "political realities" and traditions. With traditional Muslim, Greek Orthodox, and Catholic communities lining the seashore, as well as "secular" communities with a heavily polluting industrial base, the need was for "putting all this together" to arrive at a common policy.

In such a situation, he says, "you may propose an abstract ethical model, but you can't pretend that everyone is going to abide by it."

"In our daily lives, we do not live by some sort of abstract, universal code of behavior." Even the Ten Commandments, which are intended to be universal, are "rather particular" in their application to individual situations. The need, then, is to find ways to strengthen the traditional values of communities, which tend to be fairly specific, while at the same time "seeing how they can be rendered more interdependent" and universal.

The need, in other words, is for a code of ethics sufficiently general to unite different cultures, but sharply enough focused to be useful in daily life. But are there universal values that can unite different societies? "I am personally convinced that there are certain absolute norms," says Przewozny, "and these norms can even be rendered to be sufficiently applicable for certain situations." These common values, he feels, are cross-cultural. Ultimately, he says, "you should be able, no matter what background you come from, to arrive at certain absolute norms."

He admits, however, that the tendency of the modern world is toward "relative, functionalist, pragmatic models" that leave no room for "a transcendent reference." That relativism he traces back to three powerful historical influences: the growth of modern science, the development of economic theories, and the explosion of technology.

The process began, in his view, with the development of science in the seventeenth century. "Scientific research by the 1600s was completely mathematicized," he notes. Before that, he notes, science relied heavily on religious values. As it became more mathematical, however, it grew "more and more independent of other values."

Among those caught in the transition from a religious to a secular and scientific world view was Galileo, who represented "the clearest example of the total emancipation of science from other influences—he was not going to be told how to do science by theologians." Ultimately, he insulted the Pope and was punished, an outcome that, in Przewozny's view, was avoidable. Had the church leaders "been smarter," they would have said, " 'The methodologies [of science and religion] have become distinct, the competencies are distinct: let us look for some sort of interdependence, but let us respect the competencies.' "

While Przewozny has great respect for the scientific method that Galileo pursued, he nevertheless feels that it contributed powerfully to the trend toward ethical relativism. By the eighteenth century, he says, scientists had effectively eliminated religion from any "pretense" of holding overriding values. Instead, the scientists had "set themselves up above all other norms—not only independent, but telling others what the reality was."

"In other words, you no longer have a cultural value or a religious interpretation of how things are. You have only an exclusively scientific reading."

He identifies similar pressures arising historically in the second area, economics, which by the time of Adam Smith in the eighteenth century had become a discipline with "its own laws, its own principles, its own system," independent of other norms. Its interpretation of human experience, he says, was "based on the law of the marketplace, but quantified" to measure " 'how much can I give to that individual, or how much can that individual acquire.' "

"In other words, they were interpreting the common good by seeing the relation between the individual and the common in individualistic terms."

For Przewozny, that interpretation spells danger. "Individualism is destructive of social life, destructive of communal sharing, destructive of participation," he says. "The church has always maintained that the earth and its natural goods are the inheritance of all peoples." While some accuse the church on that score of communist leanings, Przewozny takes issue with that view. The church, he says, is only insisting that "there is a social obligation to private property."

"Simply because I possess the land through which a stream is flowing," he explains, "I cannot do with that stream what I want. Why? Because the fellow who has the piece of land further down the stream is dependent on my responsibility toward him. I cannot poison the stream at my point of its course, because I am damaging another individual. In other words, my property [brings with it] a social burden, a social duty, certain obligations. Most of our economic theories don't pay enough attention to this." That inattention, he maintains, is an ethical lapse, brought on by the divorce of the science of economics from moral values.

A third area that tends to inculcate relativism, he says, is technology. Since the beginnings of the industrial revolution in the nineteenth century, he says, the dominant theme of technological development has been that "what is technically feasible should be done—if you can do it technically, do it!" Under this philosophy, he says, the only limit will be "your scientific research and your money"—rather than any concept of the common good or the social value of the technology.

Over time, then, "scientific research, economics, and technology have liberated themselves, emancipated themselves from all other concerns. So what do you end up with?

A model of industrial development and industrialization that is theoretically neutral from the point of view of moral and cultural values."

Now, despite the growing recognition that local cultural and ethical values need to be respected, especially in developing nations, "this so-called western model of science, technical applications, economy, and industrialization is being applied everywhere."

The result of this "positivism and reductionism and compartmentalization," which he admits is "necessary for the scientific method," is a society "no longer open" to "absolute values." And with such values in abeyance, "most people will fall into functionalism," in which decisions concerning the future are couched only in terms of "why it should work" or "whether I can limit the damage."

Yet that functionalism, he suggests, seems to contradict the fact that, according to his figures, "85 percent of the world's population declares itself religiously affiliated."

From Przewozny's viewpoint, that religious viewpoint is the very basis for arriving at global ethical standards. Asked to define the elements of a global code of ethics, he focuses on a single concept. "One norm I think everyone would agree with is, 'Do good and avoid evil.' " On a global scale, he notes, "that is as good as you are going to get."

He notes that, when he meets with groups of religious thinkers from different faiths around the world, "I always say, 'Listen, I am going to talk to you as a Catholic, and I don't pretend that you talk to me ignoring your own background. We don't want to hear what you think we Westerners want to hear: we want to hear what you really maintain.'

And they all agree: you are supposed to do good to the other individual, you are not supposed to do evil."

This is "not just, as some philosophers have interpreted it, [a question of] 'good self-interest,' " but a basic principle of life.

One variant on this principle, he agrees, is the Golden Rule—which he interprets not only to mean "don't do what you don't want someone else to do to you," but "do good to the other individual *before* he does good to you." That rule is so widespread, he says, that it is found not only in the New Testament but "in Confucianism and in other ethical and religious systems." Despite its generality, however, it is "a very precise formulation as far as human relations are concerned."

Another variant "might be formulated this way: do all that favors life." He hastens to point out that this concept of "life-liberating action" does not ignore the food chain and the fact that "all species live off other species." It does, however, depend on the fact that, unlike other animals, "a human being is self-conscious and, therefore, subject to rights and duties or obligations." Those obligations, says Przewozny, must extend beyond humanity to other species—because, as he says, "if you destroy [the other] species you destroy yourself."

"Therefore, a life-liberating or life-fostering ethic—the principles of moral behavior in whatever you do—must increase and not reduce life. To increase life does not mean that you are not to use other species. But it does not mean that you can use them however you like for whatever is pleasant or unpleasant for you."

"There is a marvelous statement by Saint Augustine in *The City of God* in which he says, 'All things have been created without regard to human beings' convenience or inconvenience.' "

Nevertheless, Przewozny remains convinced that humans, alone among the species, have the capacity to reason and act with responsibility—a point he maintains in the face of some disagreement. When a physicist at a recent conference observed that "the DNA shows there is no substantial difference between human beings and other species," Przewozny took him on. "I said, 'Let's just remind ourselves that the DNA is an alphabet, a code. I can use a code to say what is true or what is false, and the difference between the true and the false is a qualitative difference, not just a quantitative difference.' "

He points out that "the DNA of a worm and my DNA substantially are identical. But if you move that code a fraction of a millimeter down the scale, you get a different species. I can use the twenty-six letters of the alphabet to say what is right or what is wrong, but they remain the same letters."

So, as he recalls telling the physicist, " 'if you are right and I am wrong, the next time the penguins are having a meeting on environmental pollution, invite me.' "

Is he, then, optimistic about the future of this distinct human species? "I can understand where people can be very pessimistic," he says, "when you have urban development that is completely untimed, unregulated, undisciplined. When every day you have got to send your children out to dig in garbage to find something [to eat], there is very little room for optimism."

What provides Przewozny with his optimism, however, is the level of intellectual effort now being channeled into reversing such developments and supporting environmental issues in a global context.

"One of the things that everyone should be insisting upon is that there is [such a thing as] a right to a healthy environment," he says. Then, returning to the theme of personal responsibility that has threaded itself through this interview, he notes: "That immediately means that you simply cannot do whatever you want to do."

THREE

Education and Youth
The Moral Dimension

*Humans are like that: everything they do
has a moral dimension.*

—A. H. Halsey

Graça Machel

The Dignity of the Enemy

*Personally, [forgiveness is] not easy. But
morally we cannot do anything else. This is the
only way to behave.*

For most of her life, the former first lady of Mozambique, Graça Simbine Machel, has lived in a nation at war.

Once known as Portuguese East Africa, Mozambique won independence in 1975 after a ten-year armed struggle by the Mozambican Liberation Front (known by its Portuguese acronym, Frelimo). Her husband, Frelimo leader Samora Machel, became the republic's warfare. She cites tales of children who were captured, taken back to their villages, compelled to set fire to their parents' home, and then made to shoot the parents as they tried to escape.

Her goal, she says, is to "try to make these children become children again—to do things normal children do."

Asked to elaborate on the morality of that lesson, Machel explains her convictions simply. Killing, she says, is "absolutely wrong." Revenge is not acceptable. And the values of family, community, and mutual respect are essential.

"I think especially based on my African tradition, what I would suggest is that the base of moral behavior is first of all solidarity, love, and mutual assistance—starting within the family."

Describing a nation as a "huge family built by the different cells" of individual families, she says that if a stable nation is to be created, "all of us have to look at what is happening in our families—how far we have been able to build stability, understanding, even tolerance, to accept that we can have different ideas, different positions."

Such a tolerance for diversity, she feels, is "very important. It is a question of respect for the dignity of each of us. If you have a different idea from mine, it's not because you're worse than me. You have the right to think differently."

As with individuals, says Machel, so with nations. "No one has the right to tell a country what is going to be the decision of that country but the people of that country."

But can that tolerance be stretched so far as to permit any sort of behavior—even kidnapping?

Not at all, she insists. "When you kidnap someone, you are forcing someone to do something he doesn't want to. If you were convincing him to join a movement, that would be different. But the simple fact that they have to kidnap—it's because they don't respect the other person. They feel they have the right to use other people. And of course I am against this."

One of her fundamental moral principles, in fact, is that "no one has the right to decide what other people should do." Although you can persuade, explain, and even lobby for your position, she says, "you have to give the right to somebody else to make the decision of what he wants to do. And no one has the right to impose positions through violence or force. That's why this problem of kidnapping and drugging children and teaching them to kill—this is the worst of what human beings can do to other human beings."

Even in Mozambique, she says, where killing has been common, the way forward lies through "nonviolent and nonconfrontational" means. The only way to create a sustainable nation, she insists, is to find ways to reintegrate the Renamo fighters into community life.

"We know that they have killed thousands of people in Mozambique," she explains. "But we say, 'We're not going to kill them.' We'll bring them again to society, and we'll try to make them become normal people again."

"I think one of the historic responsibilities of the oppressed is to liberate the oppressors," she says, in language echoing the Marxist orientation of the early Frelimo government. "And to reeducate them, to reorientate their minds and their behavior and to teach them to accept these moral ways of living. That's why we say, OK, come join us. We know that you made all these decisions within a system. So let us struggle together against a system which made you turn on the citizens of your country."

Is that difficult to do? Of course, Machel says. "Many families in Mozambique have lost their parents, relatives, and children. And then you go to them and you tell them, 'You have to accept that these people have to come back to your village, and you will live with them, and tomorrow they will vote with you.'"

"Personally," she says, her voice rising with feeling, "it's not easy. But morally we cannot do anything else. This is the only way to behave."

Asked about her own feelings about the death of her husband, she insists on forgiveness. "What do you expect me to do? To kill [former South African President P. W.] Botha? I'm not going to do that. I'm sure I'm not going to shake his hand. But if he's someone who will think about it, he'll understand that what he has done is really wrong. There were other solutions to the problems of differences, and not killing. And I'm giving them this alternative. I know he is different from me—we think differently. But I'm not going to kill him—I'll have to leave him alone with his feelings and thoughts."

Machel admits that it took a mental struggle for her to reach this position. "I had to talk to myself for a long time," she recalls. But what she concluded was that "I have to try to be cool. And to come to understand that maybe my message has to be to the young whites." Her own children, she says, will "have to know why their father was killed. This I have to make very clear to them. I hope in their future they will never have to be in a position to face something similar to what I had to face."

What gave her the moral strength to take this position? She traces it to two influences: her own Christian upbringing and the "core of morals and principles I learned when I joined the liberation movement."

Born in a rural area to Christian parents, she was sent at age six to a Methodist mission school where her brother and sister worked. Following secondary education in what is now Maputo, she was sent on a mission scholarship to Portugal for university studies. "I feel that was a good chance," she recalls, "because although I already had my education and was strongly against the system, being in Portugal gave me the opportunity to get in touch with people of other colonies—Angola, Guinea-Bissau, Cape Verde, San Tome. We had to pretend that we were having parties, and play the music very loud and pretend we were dancing. But we were talking about politics."

Returning home, she joined the liberation movement, where, although she received some training as a soldier, she worked with women and children and taught school near the border with Tanzania. Her views on killing were formed, she says, at that time.

"We were fighting against the Portuguese army, and of course many times many people were obliged to kill. But every time we captured a Portuguese soldier, he was not treated as [an] enemy. When he was wounded, he would be sent back [through the Red Cross]. Because we always had this sense that people can be slaves of a system, but people themselves are not bad people, and they have the same rights as we do have. So we wouldn't kill them. Our principles and our guidelines were forged when we had to face concrete problems in rural areas during the struggle."

Today, in addition to struggling to end warfare, Machel is also committed to improving the place of women in society—an issue she sees as crucial to the future of Africa. While she credits the many improvements in the status of women—including the fact that, as a woman, she herself has held government positions—she notes that change is greatly needed. In particular, the change needs to come through recognizing the particular strengths of women in three areas:

• *Culture.* "Women in our country are the thread which links generations," she says. "They are the ones who transmit, who pass along, the culture, the principles, the moral values of the society. We are a society of illiterate people. So the oral tradition is very important, because not many things can be written. And those who do [the transmitting] mostly are women."

• *Agriculture.* In addition, she says, women are the ones charged with sustaining the family. "Agriculture in rural areas is basically done by women," she explains. "So even economically they are the backbone of development."

• *Management.* Women, says Machel, are traditionally the family managers, "in the sense that they organize how to use the resources of the family."

None of that, however, means that women "have a very high social stature—because, especially in rural areas, they are strongly discriminated against by men. So one of the struggles we are trying to wage is to make the society recognize the role women are playing in the family and the role they are playing in the community and [in] the society as a whole—to recognize and to value this."

One of the central challenges, she notes, is to make the women themselves understand that they, too, have rights. "In our traditional education, women are taught specifically what are their duties, but almost nothing about their rights. So one of the things we are trying to do is to explain, to women themselves, exactly what rights they have."

What one ethical principle, today, would she single out as most important for her nation?

"I think it's respect for human life, and a strong sense of helping each other." The need at present, she says, is to recognize that "no one can do things alone—we have to do it together. We have to be able to know that when you are helping someone, you are helping yourself."

Working together, she says, will help eliminate "these very, very strong differences which exist today" between people and nations. "The science and technology have developed so much, yet there are millions and millions of people who are illiterate. I think this is the problem: how do we share the results of the development of human kind? We share it with each other in trying to reduce the terrible differences."

Derek Bok

Strengthening Individual Virtues

The zone of agreement is vast. We're arguing about exactly where the borderline is in a few fringe areas.

O f all that America has produced, little is held in higher regard around the world than its university system. Among American universities, none is older nor more prestigious than Harvard. And among university presidents, few have earned more respect from their peers and colleagues than Derek Bok, who retired in 1991 after twenty years at Harvard's helm.

A lawyer by training and a philosopher by predilection,

Derek Bok combines a relaxed joviality with a fully engaged and broad-ranging intellect. Entirely at home during an hour-long conversation beside the fireplace in his antique-filled president's office in Harvard's Massachusetts Hall, he leans back on a rose-and-green-striped sofa and rests one foot on a mahogany coffee table. He's an easy conversationalist, obviously capable of building the kind of warm, trusting relationships that, over two decades, have helped raise the university's endowment from $1 billion to $5 billion.

But let the conversation turn to one of his favorite subjects—the ethical fabric of the twenty-first century and the role of the American university in maintaining that fabric—and the depth of his thinking becomes immediately obvious.

"He is a model of what educational leadership is at its best," says Cornell University President Frank H. T. Rhodes, who has served on numerous committees with Bok. "I've never heard him speak in any but a thoughtful, balanced, perceptive, and constructive way."

"I'm an unabashed admirer of Derek Bok," adds former Columbia University President Michael I. Sovern, who singles him out as "a principled leader who has exemplified the highest values in American education."

Bok's two decades at Harvard, which began when the nation's campuses were still in turmoil over opposition to the Vietnam War, have not been without controversy. He's been criticized for not fully divesting the university of its investments in South Africa. In 1989, he lost a hard-fought battle against the unionization of the university's clerical workers. And the John F. Kennedy School of Government—established under his leadership and now preeminent in the field of public service education—still disturbs some faculty members who feel that its success has come at the expense of other, more scholarly fields.

But his towering legacy, say colleagues at Harvard and around the nation, arises in two areas: his pithy, well-researched, and widely read annual reports to the members of the Board of Overseers on various aspects of American higher education and an emphasis on moral issues that has brought ethics front and center in the Harvard curriculum.

"I think his emphasis on ethics has been a very important part of his presidency and of American education in general," says Harvard's Robert Coles, a child psychiatrist who has written widely on children's moral values and beliefs. "He's one of the few presidents who have struggled with the question of how you live up to ethics."

Bok, who did his undergraduate work at Stanford University and holds a Harvard law degree, is the author of several books, including *Beyond the Ivory Tower: Social Responsibilities of the Modern University*. He continues to write. "Life with Sissela would be intolerable if I weren't writing," he says with a rich laugh, explaining the delight he finds when both he and his wife, ethicist and author Sissela Bok, are "working on our projects at the same time."

•   •   •

In 1990, Derek Bok published a slender book titled *Universities and the Future of America*. Its central proposition was clear and direct: America's universities have failed to respond to such pressing social needs as economic competitiveness, poverty, and public education. To some, that problem might appear to be an economic or social one. To Bok, it is clearly a moral one.

"The proposition that animates the book," says Bok, "is that, in the end, efforts to respond to the kinds of public problems that I'm talking about cannot be sought only in developing the knowledge for policy solutions." Needed in addition, he says, is "a strengthening of individual virtues, ethical virtues, civic virtues on the part of individuals—especially the kinds of influential individuals who flow through our colleges and universities."

"If you just think about ideal solutions to the problem of poverty and crime and welfare and competitiveness, without worrying about the basic attitudes and dispositions of those individuals, you're probably going to fail."

Bok, who freely attributes several of his ideas to his wife, admits that it's hard to know "where ethics leaves off and civic virtue begins. One is a concern for the community, the nation, and one's sense of obligation to participate as a voter. The other is more personal—one's ethical obligations to others. But they are related. And there are a great many signs that should worry us a lot about their vitality in the country."

The university, in his view, provides an important forum for restoring that vitality, in part because college-age students are often "trying to experiment with various personas and trying to figure out what kind of a person they want to be." Bok questions whether the university is "doing enough to impress upon them that one aspect of the kind of person they want to be has to do with the degree to which they live up to moral standards."

Yet that very phrase, "moral standards," raises intellectual hackles in some parts of the scholarly world. Are there such things? Or is morality always relative, negotiable, dependent on one's own individual attitudes?

"I think relativism has really gone overboard," says Bok. "If you look at virtually all the civilizations that we have had over the past few centuries, one does find disagreements on details, but a remarkable consensus on certain basic, ethical precepts which form the foundation for a serious ethical code."

His own candidates for such a code, he says, are four in number. The first two, he says, as defined by his wife, "have to do with force and fraud: you shouldn't perpetrate violence, and you should not obtain your ends through lying and deceitful practices.

"I think the next two, which grow out of any kind of communal living, have to do with one's responsibility to keep one's promises and one's responsibility to observe laws that are laid down by agreed-upon processes."

Inherent in all four is the need for tolerance, which he defines as "a decent respect for the right of other people to have ideas, an obligation or at least a strong desirability of listening to different points of view and attempting to understand why they are held."

But such tolerance, he is quick to point out, stops short of agreeing with every idea, or even of according it "equal validity to my own" just because "some other person uttered it." Such a view, he says, entails "a sort of moral flabbiness that can be used to avoid thinking about a lot of hard questions."

"Now, all of those principles have their exceptions at the margins. There are cases where violence may be authorized, and we've got to argue about that. There are interesting boundary problems, such as self-defense. And there are cases where obeying the law gives way if the law is basically unjust."

"But as those arguments proceed about exactly where the limited exceptions are, I think we can delude ourselves into thinking, 'Gosh, you can argue about everything— everything is relative!' Actually, the zone of agreement is vast. We're arguing about exactly where the borderline is in a few fringe areas—and that's a very important debate. But it's grotesque if that persuades people that everything is relative and I can do anything I want."

That suggests, to Bok, that universities should be taking an active role in moral education. That means striking a "delicate balance" between moral education and mere indoctrination. But he insists that there are a handful of what he calls "universal principles" upon which that balance can be built.

"Nobody would regard the university as somehow transgressing that boundary if the president, faculty members, administrative bodies and so forth continue to emphasize the importance of keeping your word or not hitting your roommate. That is not regarded as indoctrination at all."

But can a modern university faculty, frequently suspicious of anything resembling absolutes, agree that there are such things as "universal principles"?

"You will always find in every community of intellectuals some people who love to play with controversial ideas, and who will try to say that everything is contextual and so forth," Bok concedes. But he adds that "the vast majority—even of the Harvard faculty—would agree with what I say: that although there may be arguments at the margin, there are fundamental working principles of ethical behavior which are important, and we're not indoctrinating our students by making a conscious effort to make them understand, appreciate, and live by those principles."

From his years of watching university faculties, Bok feels that as individuals they provide good ethical examples. He praises "the ethical behavior of faculty members in terms of elementary principles like repaying debts and being honest—perhaps because the academic life puts a very great stress on honesty in reporting, and the penalties are fairly severe."

"So I don't think there's any danger that the faculty are tearing down standards because of their own poor example—with very occasional exceptions which then one has to deal with and teach a moral lesson by the way in which one deals with them."

The problem, he explains, is that too often these opportunities for teaching moral lessons are overlooked. Those opportunities occur "in innumerable kinds of encounters that take place in the university," he says, adding that "we could do an awful lot to transform those encounters—without preaching and being censorious and stuffy—into useful moral lessons." As examples, he cites the way institutions administer rules of conduct, how they dispense financial aid and require repayment of loans, and how they coach athletic teams.

"We just haven't paid enough systematic attention to those opportunities. It's not that we do anything that's unethical—it's just that we don't do nearly as much as we might to impress on students the seriousness and the importance of this side of their lives. And that's where I think the progress can be made."

For Bok, such progress is essential. While he strongly backs the need for academic courses in moral reasoning and professional responsibility, he says they are not enough. He distinguishes between "the ability to distinguish intellectually for oneself what the right thing to do is" and "the kind of character and will to put that intellectual conclusion into practice."

"Most people who deprecate courses in moral reasoning do so by saying, 'That isn't going to make people more honest, and no one really should claim that it will.' On the other hand, even very principled people, if they're completely addled about what is right and wrong intellectually, may have the best character in the world, but the principles they're going to act on may be extremely erratic. So you need both."

Putting ethics into practice, he says, sometimes requires a resetting of priorities, a point he illustrates by citing medical research. Because medical spending has such a great "emotional hold on the American people," he says, the nation now spends $1 billion annually on cancer research—with "very few results." Much of the problem is caused by smoking. Yet the nation spends only "a few million dollars figuring out the psychology of addictions, so we can have more effective ways of getting people to stop smoking. So we do have some funny priorities."

That same sense of "funny priorities" spills over, he says, into other areas as well. "I happen to be terribly concerned about the whole range of problems associated with poverty, stunted opportunity, crime, drugs, and so forth," he says. Yet in contrast to spending for medicine, there is comparatively little research support "in the fields of education, public administration, poverty research, schools of social work."

While he notes that universities alone can't restructure the nation's priorities, he worries that educators "haven't called attention to the problem more and argued more eloquently. Our tendency has been more to take the distribution of money for granted and deploy our efforts where the money is most plentiful."

Thinking about his own career as president, he notes yet another ethical issue, which is that "success or failure is defined in part by how much money you raise, not what you raise the money for."

Often, when presidents retire, attention turns to how much money they brought to the university rather than "what really developed and how important it was—which is a very difficult question."

"And there you are, again, holding yourself hostage to the prevailing set of values in society. And it's precisely those values that account for the fact that a number of these problems exist—they are problems of neglect."

What happens if a university continues to follow the path of least resistance toward prevailing values? "You're going to be part of the problem," Bok says simply, "and not part of the solution."

Whina Cooper

Peace and Unity in Aotearoa

*I refuse to build anything that I know
is not right.*

In one sense, it's not easy to find Dame Whina Cooper. The tiny village of Panguru, New Zealand, inhabited by her Maori ancestors for several centuries, lies a day's drive and a short river-ferry crossing from Auckland, in the mountainous region of Hokianga, the Northland. The road is paved—*sealed*, in local parlance—only part of the way before turning into gravel and winding through upland meadows, sheep pastures, and forests. The house itself, set near the road beyond a hedge not far from the post office, is small and simple, almost hidden by shrubs and trees flowering in the late November spring.

In another sense, it's not at all difficult to find Dame Whina. Known throughout New Zealand simply by her first name (pronounced "*Fee*-na"), she has been described by her biographer, Michael King, as "the most visible Maori woman of her lifetime." Born in 1895 on the dirt floor of a rural cookhouse, she is the daughter of a well-known Maori leader, Heremia Te Wake, and granddaughter of a Maori mother and an American grandfather who came to New Zealand on a whaling ship in the 1830s. Called "the American Maori" by her childhood companions, she organized her first protest march at age eighteen. By the time she led the pivotal Maori Land March of 1975—in her eightieth year—she had been a gum digger, a teacher, a rugby coach, a champion rifle shot, and the founding president of the Maori Women's Welfare League. Described as a "fiery, fierce, and forceful" activist for the rights of the country's indigenous people, she is so widely respected that when the Commonwealth Games were held in New Zealand in 1990, it was her voice, and not the prime minister's, that her fellow citizens heard over the radio opening the ceremonies. Her title was conferred by Queen Elizabeth, who presented the Order of Dame Commander of the British Empire to her in 1981.

In or out of the public eye, Dame Whina sounds one theme through all that she does: the need for what she calls "peace and unity" in the country called, in her native tongue, *Aotearoa*. In a nation divided between the traditions of the Maoris—who according to legend arrived from Polynesia in seven massive canoes in the fourteenth century—and the culture of the British settlers (known as the pakeha) who came in the eighteenth century, such unity is both necessary and problematic.

Calling for adaptation of Maori traditions to keep pace with modern times, she has sometimes stood at cross-purposes with the more traditional elders of her people, especially on such matters as Maori language training, which she criticizes as having been "started in the wrong way." But she has "always been a fighter," says John Booth, a former employee of the Department of Maori Affairs assigned to the Panguru region for many years and a longtime friend and admirer. Clearly a woman used to controlling her own affairs, she maintains a lively and sometimes belligerent focus on Maori issues.

● ● ●

"The seed I would like to plant in your heart," Dame Whina wrote recently in a letter circulated to a few of her closest associates, "is a vision of Aotearoa where all our people can live in harmony. We must learn from each other and share the wisdom of each culture. We need the knowledge the pakeha brings from all over the world as well as the sense of belonging . . . of the Maori. The separate paths our people have trod can unite in a highway to the future that is built on the best of both."

Speaking English with a characteristic New Zealand accent, she begins the interview with that same focus. "I want unity," she says, adding that "God wants us to be one people."

To outsiders dealing with the Maoris, that emphasis on oneness can sometimes be frustrating, simply because to establish it often demands a great deal of ceremony and protocol. "When the Maoris start to talk," Dame Whina explains, "we always do that: we open out our hearts [to others] through relationships, to see what have *they* got, to see what kind of seed—is it the same seed, or a different seed?"

Despite fundamental differences between the pakeha and Maori culture, she remains convinced that, at bottom, there is a core of sameness, and that the Maoris must, as she says, "look back to appreciate the past, but look forward to advance."

The balance of past and future, in fact, is a point of increasing concern for her. She is acutely aware that "the elders are all dead" and that she is now "left alone, and the demands seem to be greater." As a repository for the past wisdom of her culture, she has great respect for what she calls the "commonsense" traditions, a point that emerges with some vehemence when she talks about the need to pay more attention to raising children.

"Te ihi te mana te tapu," she says in Maori, words that for her connote "the sacred path of a person, of what is left to us by our forefathers," and the need to "do the right thing, plant the right thing."

"We know what was left by our forefathers," she insists, "but are we doing it? We're not. We don't know what we are, at present." She worries that the present generation—visible next door, where a young Maori washes his car to the raucous sounds of Western rock and reggae blaring from a boom-box—has "no ears" and "nothing up here" inside the head.

"I keep saying, 'This is God's country! Only, we the people running it must be doing something wrong.' "

While it might be expected that someone of her age and stature would seek answers in a wholesale return to her traditions, Dame Whina has little patience with such attitudes. She worries, instead, that her people are "too much going backwards."

"I can't be bothered with a lot of backward people," she snaps. "I want to go into the future."

To illustrate, she tells of a recent visit to her home by a group of young Maori students who had built a fleet of traditional canoes. "The schools were helping make them—carving, and everything—and they wanted to learn how to paddle." They were arranging a great festival in which canoes from all over the Northland would assemble in the river near Panguru, and they had come to ask Dame Whina to open the day's ceremonies.

"They all sat down there," she says, pointing around her small living room crowded with chairs, "and some of the elders, and I put the question, 'Hey, you people coming here, what for?' And they said, 'We want you to open the day for this paddling.' "

" 'What progress can you see in what you're asking me to open up?' " she asked them. When they couldn't answer, she set them a startling challenge.

" 'I've got a patch of kumara,' " she told them, referring

to the common New Zealand sweet potato, " 'about forty ton. I want those kumara to be shipped away. I think I can get a good price for them in England. Now, I want you to put it on your canoe to take it to England.' "

"And they looked around at each other, because they knew how big their canoes are and how rough the sea is. And I said, 'Have you got the answer for that?' They said, 'No, no, no!'

"I said, 'Here is the answer: you come here and say, "Whina, I don't think we could manage to take your kumara.' " That's what you're going to say. Now, if you came here and said to me, 'Whina, we need your help . . .' What is this? Education! I'm at your service.

"I told these children, 'I want you to learn about a nail, a screw, all the carpentry things—I want you to say, 'I want to know what all these things can do to build a big ship to load your forty ton, Whina.' Then I'd say, 'Good boys, that's the way! A little canoe, what can you do with it?— and your mind be as little as that!' "

In the end, she recalls, she refused to open those ceremonies. "I wouldn't," she says, "because *I refuse to build anything that I know is not right*—to build those young people with something that is not right."

Over the years, she says, she has often been at odds with some of her fellow Maoris over such stands. What has sustained her, she says, is the Christian faith in which she, like so many Maoris, was raised.

"I had a dream over forty years ago," she says. "I dreamed I wanted to go to heaven. So I went. As I was standing, waiting for the Lord [Jesus] to come, he got nearer to me, and I saw his eyes—whew—strong! And he asked me, 'Whina, what do you want?' I said, 'Lord, please, I want to come to heaven.'

"And he turned and said, 'Whina, there's *much more* for you to do!' "

That experience gave her the courage to accept positions which, she says, she never could have hoped to fulfil—and to carry them out despite a lack of advanced education and a background as a simple villager.

Shortly after that dream, she recalls, she was appointed by the government to head a new organization known as the Maori Women's Welfare League, a position that would require her to travel throughout the nation meeting women. When she returned home from the appointment ceremony, she recalls falling on her knees in front of a statue of the Virgin Mary—a statue that still stands beside her chair in her home in Panguru—and praying.

" 'You are the mother of our Lord,' " she recalls saying. " 'Would you like to be my mother, too? To teach me, to tell me what to do, please—because they appointed me to do this work, and I don't know how to start. So can you help me, please?' "

"From that day," she recalls, "I have not been disappointed—because it seems to me I have risen from down at the bottom. And who can I thank but God for doing the right thing—because I am nothing."

Now, long after her work with the Welfare League, she still retains active ties to women's organizations—sometimes to their dismay. Opening a recent conference in Kaitaia, she lambasted women for ignoring their children to pursue their own pleasures. Of particular concern to her was what she describes as the pakeha habit of bottle-feeding babies.

"I told all those women, 'What are these for?' " she says, gesturing toward her breasts. " 'You've left off to feed your baby. Your baby needs that, to know that you are the mother, not a mother in a bottle. You've followed the pakeha style: never mind about the baby, get a bottle, put the milk inside, get yourself a beautiful dress, buy a hat, dress yourself up!' "

The result, she told them, is that the news media is full of accounts of Maori children going wrong and turning to crime and delinquency. " 'Whose fault?' " she asked the women. " 'You, the mother, because you keep saying, "those children won't listen." Why not? It's your duty to feed them, to [let them] know you're the mother.' "

Outdoors, the noon air is full of bird songs. Dame Whina's nephew serves tea—including fried fish, kumara, and cake—and someone recalls that, this being November 26th, it is Thanksgiving Day in the United States. That reminds Dame Whina of her Yankee roots and of her half-American father, who taught her the rudiments of hospitality.

"My father said, 'If you see any strangers going past, you call them—*Kia Ora*'—that means to call them to come here. And I said, 'Dad, I might not have anything in my cupboard.' And he said to me, 'See this water running from that mountain in this big creek? It costs you nothing. You go and get that water and boil it for that visitor. He'll appreciate what you did.' "

"Ever since I've been doing that—my family does that, the whole of this place," she says.

As her visitors are leaving, she calls for a pen, inscribes her name on her last copy of the letter she recently wrote to her friends, and gives it to them. Not surprisingly for one so interested in the future, the letter closes with a soaring injunction to "accept the responsibility for nurturing our children."

"We must guard our children's growth as carefully as a commercial gardener looks after his crop that will provide his wealth," she wrote. "We must shelter them from the wind of neglect, we must cull the weeds that choke their brains with the rubbish, we must water and feed their minds with a sound education.

"Take care of our children.

"Take care of what they hear.

"Take care of what they see.

"Take care of what they feel.

"For how the children grow, so will be the shape of Aotearoa.

"We must all be diligent gardeners."

A. H. Halsey

Dialects of a Common Language

*The beginning of turning things around so
that the species can survive is to be found
precisely in the search for universal values. We
must take it much more seriously than we do.*

sk A. H. Halsey where he learned his ethics, and he points straight back to his childhood. The son of a railway driver from Kentish Town and of a mother from the London Irish, he recalls his own upbringing as based on "truth and love—caring about human beings, and telling it as it is."

"I was lucky enough to have a mother who said to me at the earliest stages, 'Don't give me no soft soap: that is not what it's like, child—look at it again!' I've always thought of this sort of mother figure as being outraged by offenses against the truth."

The lesson that came home to him from that upbringing, he says, is that "you're always going to make mistakes if you deceive yourself."

An engaging speaker with a warm and ready smile, he is now professor of social and administrative studies at Oxford University and a fellow of Nuffield College. Widely regarded as the leading proponent of a school of thought known as ethical socialism, he is coauthor (with Norman Dennis) of *English Ethical Socialism: Thomas More to R. H. Tawney,* which traces ethical socialism from the fourteenth to the twentieth century. Describing it as "a moral and political tradition which we believe to be the best available guide to a good life for our children," the authors find that it consists of "six common factors."

> First, second, and third are positive commitments to fraternity, liberty, and equality. Fourth is . . . the rejection of the 'historicist' view that a society's future is ineluctable and will be the result of social laws working themselves out with an iron necessity toward an inevitable goal. Fifth, nevertheless, is a sense of the enormous contribution that a society's past makes to its present morality and institutions. . . . Sixth is a shared belief in the power of moral character to perfect a person and ennoble a nation [p. 5].

An engaging and popular speaker, he is known for his ability to make the insights of scholarship understandable to broad audiences. "We asked him to give the address at our annual general meeting," says David French, head of the British marriage guidance council Relate, "because it was fascinating that someone of his intellectual background and allegiances should be so concerned for the role of families."

"A. H. Halsey is perhaps our most distinguished sociologist," says Donald Trelford, former editor of the prestigious London Sunday newspaper the *Observer*, "consistently challenging over two generations, never afraid to state his own values but always ready to adapt his conclusions to the facts unearthed by his own and others' research." Halsey lives with his wife and family in Oxford.

● ● ●

"The essence of the common ethic," observes A. H. Halsey in a kind of summary statement of his outlook, "lies somewhere in linking a personal ethic, a personal morality, a personal set of beliefs, to circumstances."

For Halsey, that last word is crucial. Although he is well aware that ethics often finds its articulation in soaringly abstract principles, he is clear that it finds its relevance only in down-to-earth experiences. As though to enforce his point, the interview he grants on the subject takes place partly in the quiet of his book-strewn ground-floor office, opening onto the courtyard of his college—and partly across facing seats on a British Rail train whisking him to London amid a rabble of children's and adult's voices.

In Halsey's view, the "ethical heroes" whose lives are most instructive are those who are "committed to doing the best they can in whatever circumstances—who never lose their sense that, however bad the circumstances, they are morally responsible." Whatever the ethical, cultural, or religious tradition, he says, that commitment defines the ethical individual.

The English, in his view, have a long history of such moral commitment in the face of adversity. So pronounced is that ethical tradition, in fact, that it becomes kind of English "exceptionalism"—taking form, as he says with a wry chuckle, in their strong belief that "if God wanted to say something terribly important about any of the great [global] issues, it would be a sort of habit of the Almighty to reveal the message first to an Englishman." While that centuries-old attitude may produce particular faults of pride and self-assurance, he notes that "you can rely on these people to pursue a particular moral line: whatever the government says, whatever anybody else says, it's something for which they are responsible because they are connected straightforwardly to God Almighty."

It is that sense of responsibility that most defines, for Halsey, the common ethic of the future. "It is an ethic that says: we are responsible for our grandchildren, and we will make [the world] easier or more difficult for our grandchildren to be good people by what we do right here and now."

No matter how large the issues—global population, environmental degradation, the gap between the developing and the industrial world—he insists that "you're never going to solve those problems in any serious way without a moral dimension. Why is that? Because humans are like that: everything they do has a moral dimension."

That moral dimension—that taking of responsibility—depends on striking the right balance between the overarching ideas of the social conscience and the practical impulses of individualism. In Halsey's view, the balance has recently gotten skewed. "On the whole, I would say that individualism has been the dominant virtue over the last generation."

In the political realm, that emphasis has led to some unreasonable expectations, particularly in America, where the popularity of Bill Clinton arises in part from the belief that a strong individual can change the entire course of a society. Halsey is unconvinced. "Don't forget that the picture of mankind is like playing a game of cards with an enormous pack: each card will move the game a little bit—some more than others—but any individual one is not very strong. Things tend to move according to the last play."

Yet because each card matters, "the way the individual behaves is absolutely crucial, because he can either make life easier for his grandchildren or make it worse for them."

Recently, he says, "we've been living through a worse period, not a good period."

Among the things that make it worse, he says, are the "lies, manipulations, and pretenses" that governments impose on their publics. More serious and subtle, however, is ethical relativism, which he sees "creeping in all over the place, especially in universities." Insisting that all ethics is relative—that there are no basic standards or values except as people imagine them—this viewpoint is, in Halsey's mind, closely allied with "all this stuff about deconstructionism, postmodernism, and certain forms of feminism," which are all "denials of the possibilities of saying somebody's better than somebody else." The universities, he says, are "actually paying people high salaries to teach that to the young"—leading students to conclude that there is "no way in which you can make moral discriminations" and hence no need for ethics. Carried to its logical extreme, he says, that kind of teaching betokens "the end of civilization."

Yet Halsey is also aware of some pointers suggesting that society's moral barometer may not be falling as dangerously as some think. First, he notes, "there's always the phenomenon that 'things aren't like they used to be' "—a tendency he calls "old people's nostalgia." Second, he says that "standards of honesty and fair play and compassion" have not sunk "right down to the bottom." If you listen to children these days, he says, "it is amazing how often you find serious altruistic impulses being expressed by them—and I mean serious ones, not just the easy stuff."

What, then, must be done to help move the moral barometer upward?

"I'd like to say first what you shouldn't do, [which] is to say, 'We've got to go back to wisdom and caring, and therefore you must go to Sunday School next Sunday.' It's no use trying to turn the clock back."

Turning to positive answers, he points to three necessary activities. First, he says, "there are certain conditions that will raise the probability of good behavior, modest behavior, caring behavior, and [you should take] every opportunity you have—and you have thousands every day—to impose the conditions for moral behavior on the people you attend to. To put it in economic terms: you try to reduce the price of decency wherever you can."

The second necessity, he says, is "to recognize that a good deal of inhumanity in the world stems from ignorance, and so if you want to do the positive thing you should spread knowledge."

"One of the things that really upsets me is the knowledge that while we rely so much on having a democratic way of life in the Anglo-Saxon countries, we don't teach it. Most of these kids don't even know what committee procedures are. They don't have any idea of exactly what it means to say that we should have a voice in our own future. We don't teach a curriculum of democratic civics and democratic practice which would habituate individuals to the social mechanisms for maximizing the good and minimizing the bad."

"Knowledge," he insists, "is the precondition for good morals: get the facts right, don't tell fairy stories." The more sophisticated you become about economics, for example, the more you understand "just why it is that the North manages to exploit the South. Why are Africans starving in their villages? Because they are placed in a set of economic relations with other parts of the earth that give them the capacity [for] reducing their death rates, but don't teach them how to enter markets on even terms with the people who are buying their primary products." In that context, he says, the only moral solution is "to get to a higher knowledge base."

Beyond knowledge, however, lies a third necessity, which he describes as "attention to ritual." Millions of our ancestors, he notes, have repeated the catechism, or the decalogue, or some "rigmarole" that reminds you that "eating people is wrong, all that sort of stuff."

"I'm joking about it, in a way," he says, "but a lot of the ritual of life is a reminder of the moral and ethical verities." In primitive societies, he points out, there typically occurs a kind of "Sunday school ritual at adolescence in which they teach males and females what is good and what is bad sexually, and what the gods have said, and make them [into] moral affirmations."

While the danger of such moral affirmations is that they can lead to "the Ku Klux Klan and tribalism, wife burning and all that," they are "nonetheless an important part of the moral formation of individuals," leading them to "identify themselves with entities much bigger than themselves."

Ritual and knowledge, however, figure largely in the debate over a modern tendency that Halsey finds troubling: fundamentalism in its various political, social, and religious forms.

"The fundamentalist religions are in some ways a reaction against our modern world," he says. "They want to get back to an earlier world." One of the marks of that earlier world is a kind of innocence, or lack of knowledge, which is held to be so strongly allied to goodness that "saintliness is almost made coincidental with ignorance."

While that may be dangerous, it is at the very least understandable. "There is a form of discipline toward others, even a decency toward others, which comes out of the period of history in which most people were absolutely innocent." The impulse of fundamentalism, then, is to retain such a core of values in the face of a world in which "we've been forced in all sorts of ways to make knowledge, particularly of the natural world, much more widespread. The jobs people do, the way people procreate, requires them to know more about the natural world."

Where do those core values come from? Halsey points to the world's great religions, which he describes as "simply dialects of a common language."

"When you go through the sacred writings, it's incredible the extent to which there is enormous agreement as to what the ideals are that people should follow." The Ten Commandments, he says, constitute "as good an expression as anything else" of this commonality: leaving aside the four "churchy and ritualistic requirements" with which they begin, the remaining six "moral injunctions—no killing, no stealing, not coveting your neighbor's wife, and so on—are repeated over and over again in the other sacred writings." He concludes that "there are more commonalities than differences in the moral outlook of the major religions."

And while he is impressed by "increasing signs that people think they can be more efficient in the satisfaction of the wants of others if they are 'moral' than if they are not," he recognizes the difficulty of adapting the overarching moral precepts in a specific context. That difficulty, however, does not mean that the Commandments, or the central principles of the other religions, should be tossed aside as unworkable. "You're always going to run into contextual difficulty. But that is in no way an argument" against the principles. The way forward, he notes, is through "appealing to the absolutely fundamental things—because they are consensual, not contextual," deriving their authority not from the case-by-case details so much as from the fact that they represent shared agreement.

As for individual lives, so for nations, where the concept of an ethical foreign policy is often derided. "The possibility of nations having *morals* rather than *interests* is something that exists—even though the actual record is one much more of interests rather than morals."

Is ethics, then, a survival issue for the next century?

"Absolutely, unequivocally yes," replies Halsey. The reason, he says, is simply the growth of the scale of our communities. Throughout history, he explains, most people have lived permanently in very small communities, so that "most human beings have been produced after interactions with about 150 people" from which mates were selected. "Now we're living in a world where 150 has become 150 million."

"The impact round the world of something that happens in a remote suburb of southern California called Hollywood, or of an argument between two different nationalities in Russia or Yugoslavia, draws in the whole world in a way that couldn't have been done before." The great religions, he notes, anticipated this global contact with the moral doctrine that "everyone is your neighbor." But until now that had been a kind of ideal.

"We are now actually in those conditions," he says. "So it is a [question of] survival. The beginning of turning things around so that the species can survive is to be found precisely in the search for universal values. We must take it much more seriously than we do."

Jill Ker Conway

Women, Children, and Ethics

*Young ones learn their ethics from the adult
generation. So we have to model a greater
ethical concern.*

I n her autobiography, *The Road from Coorain,* Australian
author and feminist historian Jill Ker Conway describes
her upbringing on the arid western grasslands of New
South Wales. "Here," she writes, "pressed into the earth
by the weight of that enormous sky, there is real peace. To
those who know it, the annihilation of the self, subsumed
into the vast emptiness of nature, is akin to a religious
experience. . . . What was social and sensory deprivation

for the stranger was the earth and sky that made us what we were."

It was an environment, she remembers, that especially affected the women who lived there. "The ideal woman," she writes, "was a good manager—no small task with only wood stoves, kerosene lamps, inadequate water, and the nearest store for canned goods fifty to a hundred miles away. She was toughened by adversity, laughed at her fears, knew how to fix things which broke in the house, and stifled any craving she might once have had for beauty. . . . Everyone knew the most important gift to a child was an upbringing which would toughen him (her) up so as to be stoic and uncomplaining about life's pains and ready for its reverses."

When Conway graduated from the University of Sydney in 1958 and left for America, that background enabled her to become "a good manager"—both of her own scholarly work on social and intellectual history and ultimately of Smith College, where she served as president for ten years. Having received her Ph.D. from Harvard, and having taught at the University of Toronto, she is now visiting scholar and professor in MIT's Program in Science, Technology, and Society. She lives with her husband in Milton, Massachusetts.

● ● ●

It is snowing into the shrubbery outside her colonial living room as Jill Ker Conway ushers a visitor in. She apologizes for jet lag: she has just returned to this Boston suburb from Australia, where shooting is in progress for a film based on

132

her autobiography. As the discussion turns to the values and ethics needed to shape a sustainable future, it is apparent that her Australian background is never far from her conversation.

First on her list, she says, is a need to reshape the role of women in societies around the world. "As we bring new technologies to our Western societies and undermine traditional patterns of agriculture and family and domestic life," she says, "what we see happening is an increasing exploitation of women and children and increasing violence against them—combined with a kind of international trade in women for sexual exploitation that makes Victorian prostitution look like small beer."

The examples she cites girdle the globe. "There is a trade in women in Saudi Arabia. Women are sold into prostitution in Thailand, Cambodia, and Burma. Everybody knows about the Japanese [sex-tourism] bonanza affecting the Philippines and many parts of Southeast Asia. That is a terrible blot on civilization."

She acknowledges that the problem has long historical precedent. But her conversations with Asian and African women point to a serious escalation in recent years. "As men go away to work in mines, as they do in Africa—or as women are shipped off to the city as surplus, as happens in many parts of rural Asia—the community constraints on violence against them are eroding." She notes, too, that the revival of traditional customs in the Islamic and Hindu worlds subject wives who are no longer wanted to "accidental-but-on-purpose household fires." In India, she says, "it happens with the arranged marriage: the bride is sent home to her family to bring back a transistor radio or television, and the family knows that, if she does not produce it, there will be a fire and she will die."

She also notes "an escalating problem of violence against women" in the developed world, but says that it is "nothing like" the scale of the problem in the developing world. In those countries, the issue takes on added significance because of its relation to global population. "There is plenty of evidence to show that, wherever women get control over the returns on their own work, they allocate them so that the health of their children increases and so they won't have to have so many [children]."

"That is a new problem," she insists, "which I wish I could get more feminists in the United States and the West to be concerned about."

The second values-driven issue on her list is concern for the global environment. "I am not of the school that blames corrupt corporate management for the degradation of the environment," she says. "I think that we each personally have to change our habits of consumption—and that if we did that, there would be an instant response from profit-making enterprises."

She dismisses the argument that "we are all dupes of consumerism" who "can't change our habits [even] if we wish to." Such changes, in fact, are already beginning. Her current students at MIT, both male and female, are "willing to change their standards of consumption for two purposes: to be better environmental citizens, and to achieve greater equity between the sexes." What unites these two points of view in this post-1960s generation, she feels, is the fact that these students "see exploitation of the environment and of human beings as on a continuum of the same set of values."

Conway's third point centers on what she calls "north-south inequity"—the problem of the severe and growing economic imbalance between the wealthy developed nations that generally lie in the temperate northern hemisphere and the predominately tropical and southern less-developed countries. While the evidence of inequity is increasingly apparent, she says she is disturbed by the simplistic arguments used by some in the north who say that " 'those people should control their birth rate' or 'why should we be expected to invest our tax money in achieving a more stable human environment for non-Western countries?' "

"I just came back from a board meeting of a major international service company," she says. "Everybody knows the world is one world: they trade twenty-four hours a day in many different currencies, and you would not have to persuade anybody there that we live in a single global environment. But when I go out to dinner in a suburb like this, it is not apparent to people at all."

And while she acknowledges that a great deal of the West's foreign-aid contributions have "ended up in the hands of governments or corrupt contractors who are not the appropriate beneficiaries," that does not convince her that "we should slack off in the slightest in trying to achieve some global transfers of one kind or another."

What does she see as the risks of not doing so?

The danger, she says, is no longer of global warfare, since "mass warfare between nation-states" is increasingly seen as an ineffective tool of policy. The danger, instead, will come from "the kind of terrorism and sporadic but well-targeted violence that is not inspired by sinister international conspiracies but by the kind of desolation and desperation that gives you one kind of urban guerrilla army in Lima, Peru, and another terrible terrorist army in the rural areas." Peru, she says, is "a society which has no hope—although theoretically it could be another California and feed the hemisphere."

How can those three broad issues—the woman's place, environmental degradation, and the north-south divide—best be addressed?

The problems, Conway admits, defy simple answers. The growth of technological systems—whether they are "systems of ideas or of material objects"—has produced a world "so complex and complicated that it is impossible to imagine any oversight by professionals" to assure the proper functioning of large-scale systems. "There isn't really that much supervision of how professionals in the high-tech world behave," she notes, citing as evidence "the fact that we have gone for so many years implanting various kinds of defective mechanisms into the human body" for medical reasons. The same problem applies, she says, "across the spectrum" in law, government, psychiatry, engineering, and scientific research in general.

Nor does she think the problem of regulation can ever be addressed simply through legal structures. "I can't imagine ever inventing the *regulated* free environment that would control how somebody builds a bridge, or the decisions those people made about the Challenger O-rings, and so on. In the long run, the only way a society can control [those issues] is ethical."

How, then, do you raise a society's ethical barometer?

"I think there are probably three ways," she says, speaking as an educator. First, she says, it is clear that "young ones learn their ethics from the adult generation. So we have to model a greater ethical concern."

Second, she notes, is a need for more volunteerism by the young. Educators could "broaden people's social conscience" and help impart a "stronger social service orientation in them" if they would only insist on "some form of public service between high school and college or college and graduate school" and "some exposure to society's problems."

Even today, she says, she still meets people whose "lives were changed by being part of the New Deal or the CCC [Civilian Conservation Corps]" and whose careers were shaped by that experience. By contrast, she says, "society demands no service from young people today. It is very meritocratic in the way it goes about things. We finance everybody's education through debt—and one of the consequences is that very early young people learn to think about themselves as an 'investment' that is going to 'pay off.' It is fascinating to see that the people who do most brilliantly in this educational system are the children of immigrants who don't think that way."

The third point, says Conway, centers on something approaching a religious sensibility. "It's very hard to say this without sounding like somebody from the New Right," she observes, "but I think that in some ways a totally secular education for young people may not develop a formed conscience." It doesn't matter, she says, whether you are going to be "a believer in later life" or not. The fact is, she says, that "a sense of evil and personal guilt and the obligation to see to one's moral well-being is a religious mentality, and we do not foster that at all."

She recognizes that such a religious outlook can be "subject to all kinds of misuse and manipulation" in a world that is "menaced by fundamentalism of many different kinds—Muslim, Hindu, Arab, and the fundamentalist Right in our own society." But the absence of such a religious mentality "is also a terrible social hazard." And in fact, she adds, "those kinds of fundamentalism are there" because today's limited versions of moral consciousness "leave out something very important."

But can a genuinely broad moral consciousness be developed through a public education system, given the nature of today's pluralistic and diverse society? "The Roman Empire managed to do it," she says, noting that "until it was suddenly undermined by Christianity, it had this great structure of tolerance" for a wide variety of religious practices. So too did the Islamic empire under Akbar, who settled India and "prided himself on tolerating and supporting other religious minorities." Today, however, she worries that the trend may be moving in the opposite direction. "Many of the things that we choose to call 'ethnic tension' often have religious roots," she says.

What, then, is the connection between religion and ethics? Can there be ethics without faith?

"In my view," she says, "you probably can't have a strong ethical sense without some first principles." Some societies find those first principles in a connection to the land: Australian Aboriginals, she says, "believe the earth is sacred and that when you go to visit the place where your father's tribe walked, you kiss the ground and embrace the dust." Western cultures, too, have such first principles, although they are no longer as consciously held. In the West, she says, "we have really been living off the moral capital of the Judeo-Christian world, while the religious system that produced that set of ethical values erodes away."

That erosion, she believes, has laid the foundation for the growth of fundamentalism in many developing societies, where religious leaders have "often devised the most rigid and authoritarian notions of their traditional religion" in order to "expunge the West and de-Westernize the society." Islam, for instance, is nothing like the faith that "the Islamic fundamentalists are insisting upon today."

Where, then, does she see the future taking us?

Her answer begins with a backward reflection. "The old missionary world of the eighteenth and nineteenth centuries," she says, "cared a lot about what happened in other parts of the planet—especially in societies they defined as heathen. Even in the first blush of idealism after the Second World War, people looked outward from this society and felt an obligation to share some wealth and resources." But with the Vietnam War came "the total disaster of the misdirection of those concerns," leaving people feeling that "we can't do anything right in our relationship with other societies, so we will forget it."

Today, she says, her hope comes from "a revival of internationalism, more rooted in an environmental sense. One can't begin to care about the environment without caring about the pressures on people that lead them to damage it more than it is. So perhaps there is the possibility of a nonimperialist concern about other parts of the world."

Can that happen? She admits that "a quick look at the electoral politics of the United States does not give you much optimism for the future." Then her features break into a wry smile. "But not having been born here," she says, "I don't think of [the United States] as the center of the globe. It might occur elsewhere."

FOUR

Entrepreneurs and the Economy
Pie for the Grandchildren

If you promise pie in the sky, that's hard to check up on. But if you promise pie for the grandchildren, and the grandchildren turn up and there's no pie, the whole thing's over.

—Kenneth Boulding

Muhammad Yunus

Peeling Off the Differences

If the political will is created, I see the
tendency toward the complete elimination of
poverty in the future. We can clean this whole
mess up in one decade.

One day in 1974, in a poverty-wracked village in Bangladesh, Muhammad Yunus stumbled upon a woman making bamboo stools—and upon a new concept of banking that would eventually lift millions of people in developing nations out of abject poverty.

Professor Yunus, who then headed the economics department at Chittagong University, recalls what impelled him to walk through the village that day: a famine so intense that people were dying in the street, and a frustration with theories of economics that seemed utterly irrelevant to such a disaster.

Speaking the woman's dialect, he asked about the difficulties she was having. The problem, he quickly learned, was that she had no bamboo of her own. So she was forced to borrow money to buy it from a trader, who then required her to sell the finished product back to him at whatever price he offered.

"She made only two pennies for a whole day's work," Yunus recalls. "But she could improve her economic situation if someone would give her the five takas [about fifteen U. S. cents] she needed to buy bamboo."

Yunus lent her the money, and he came back the next day with a student to help him find others like her. By the end of the week they had identified forty-two people who, if given very small loans, could begin to become financially independent. Total amount needed: the equivalent of twenty-six U. S. dollars.

Feeling "shocked and ashamed" to be part of a society that could not provide $26 to "forty-two able, willing, eager, hard-working, skilled workers," he recalls that his impulse was to take the money from his own pocket. "But I realized that was an emotional response, not a solution."

Out of that realization, and after nine years of battling the bureaucracies and the paperwork of his country's banking system, came a concept known as microenterprise lending—though Yunus prefers the term "*microcredit* lending." Out of it, too, came the birth of the Grameen Bank, the first bank in the world to specialize in tiny loans to people with no collateral and no credit history.

Now operating in twenty-nine thousand villages in Bangladesh, the bank has $40 million in savings deposits, loans $10 million a month, and serves 1.3 million borrowers, 92 percent of whom are women. The loans, averaging $75, have an astonishingly high repayment rate of 97 percent, and this from people with no property to pledge against a possible default, and for whom the loan itself is almost always the first time in their lives they had ever touched money.

"The idea of a credit program for the poor was always there," says Yunus. But it was typically associated with religious organizations. "To see it as a banking practice, a business proposition—nobody dared even to think about it!" Similar programs are now mushrooming up in other countries, including the United States, where microcredit lending is proving successful among the Cherokee tribe in Oklahoma and the Sioux in South Dakota.

Yunus, who earned his doctorate in economics from Vanderbilt University, was born in 1940 of illiterate parents in what was then British India. Now, as managing director of the Grameen Bank in Dhaka, he is a widely sought-after speaker and consultant in international circles. A member of the board of trustees of the International Rice Research Institute in the Philippines, he holds honorary degrees from the University of East Anglia in the United Kingdom and from Oberlin College in the United States. He was recipient of the Aga Khan Award for Architecture in 1989 and the

Humanitarian Award from CARE (Cooperative for American Relief Everywhere, Inc.) in 1993.

• • •

When Muhammad Yunus looks ahead into the twenty-first century, he sees "a complex, fast-changing world which is getting used to dumping long-held sacred values, ideas, and institutions in a matter of days and weeks, rather than decades and centuries."

Yet there must be, he insists, "something in human beings which transcends everything, which defines [their] ultimate destiny." Asked to identify what he calls the "common ethical threads" that will bind humanity in the twenty-first century, he points to five ideas: oneness, truth, human rights, freedom from poverty, and the collapse of central authority.

• *Oneness.* In the future, says Yunus, "the oneness of humanity is the basic ethical thread that will hold us together. All kinds of differences and differentiations will either peel off by deliberate decision or by the march of events. People will forget that one is a black, a white, a Bangladeshi, an American. These will be [merely] historical identities."

That change, he says, has already begun. The phenomenon of people and nations "falling backwards" into poverty, he says, will end. Already, he notes, nations that thirty years ago were languishing in economic backwaters—he mentions Korea and Taiwan—"all of a sudden are equal with advanced nations." Even such tough cases as Nigeria and Liberia, he says, will be uplifted by "the march of events."

"If we can hold on to the oneness, this will be the common theme for people discovering equality among people."

• *Truth.* Given the advances of technology, Yunus argues that we will no longer be able to "outsmart each other by a play of words, because information will become so obvious and so vivid." Even in Bangladesh—which, with a population half the size of the United States crammed into an area equivalent to Florida, is "probably *the* poorest country in the world"—the nation's single television channel has just begun carrying the Cable News Network from 7 A.M. to 5 P.M. "Any home you go by in Bangladesh," he says, "they know what's going on in America."

In the past, he says, "nations cheated nations by keeping secrets; people cheated people by keeping secrets." Diplomacy, he argues, was defined as "how carefully you can keep your secrets, and at the same time feel that you're doing the right thing."

In the future, by contrast, "it will be difficult to play around with information. People will be forced to reveal themselves. Nothing can be kept hidden or secret—not in computers, not in the halls of government, nothing. People will feel much more comfortable when they're dealing in truth. You converge around and in truth."

• *Human rights.* For Yunus, human rights include freedom of speech, the right to food and shelter and to health and education. Included also is what he calls "the right to credit."

Needed, he says, are lending institutions that don't ask for a credit reference, a driver's license, or any of the things that typically keep the poor from borrowing. As a banker, he longs to see a world in which "the fact that you're a human being, that you can shake hands with me and tell me your name, means you're entitled to borrow from me." The point, he says, is to "design an institution that can deal" with such transactions.

Standing in the way, he insists, are financial institutions designed for the past but still active today. "You can't bring them into the jet age," he says, because "they still maintain the philosophy" of the age that created them. He foresees a steady collapse of such institutions, likening them to the Berlin Wall, which was not really designed by anyone and eventually simply "peeled off piece by piece" until it disappeared.

"When the large banks fall apart, when Citibank Corporation falls apart, people will be happy and will say, 'This thing controlled our life: it has to go.' "

As that happens, "new institutions which we don't know will emerge." Along the way, however, an ethical framework will be needed to keep the human rights issues together. If we fail to pay attention to that ethical framework, he says, "then probably these things will not happen, [and things will] go on their merry way."

• *Freedom from poverty.* The more humanity clings to its human rights, the more "the question of poverty will become important." The reason: "poverty is the name for the denial of all human rights."

In the future, he says, the alleviation of poverty will be driven by two forces. The first will be a sense of shame, as people around the world begin asking, " 'Why should any human being starve?' "

"People will feel very uncomfortable that anybody has to starve, anybody has to be shelterless, anyone has to die of diseases that are such curable things. That feeling will grab people."

The second force will be the recognition that everyone is benefited by a reduction of poverty—since the poor create international conflicts, destroy the environment for their own survival, and eat up everything in sight "like big gangs of pests in Africa."

To illustrate, Yunus sets an example. "You're poor, I'm rich," he says. "I'm producing shoes, but you cannot buy my shoes, so I cannot sell my shoes. It's in my interest that your financial position is such that you can buy my shoes. But if one billion people around the world are living in abject poverty, that means they're out of the market. If I can bring them up, I have a big market waiting for me."

The ethical issue, he notes, is simply "how long we should tolerate hunger and poverty." There is no necessary reason, he says, why poverty must exist. Nor is it all that complicated to address. "It's not technology that's needed, it's not resources—it doesn't take that much resource. It comes back to will. If the political will is created, I see the tendency toward the complete elimination of poverty in the future. We can clean this whole mess up in one decade."

149

• *The collapse of central authority.* As communication brings humanity closer to living in a global village, Yunus predicts that "central authorities will crumble." Replacing them will be "information dissemination bodies," enabling individuals to have "strength in themselves."

The global village he has in mind will not have "a central headquarters with all kinds of gadgets controlling every part of the world and a central computer keeping everybody's information. I don't think that's the kind of world we'd like to build." Instead, he foresees frameworks designed "to let people do things their own way, to be fulfilled in their own way," based on technologies that will allow you to have "information at the tip of your pen" about anything in the world.

Such developments, he feels, will lead away from institutions that hoard information and toward a greater dissemination of ideas. It will also lead people more frequently to ask such large philosophical questions as, " 'Why live? What is the meaning of life? What are we trying to achieve? What is the fulfillment that we want to get to?' "

But given the state of the world, with its wars and racial animosities and economic divides, can these five elements be realized?

"I'm very hopeful," says Yunus. It will not happen "because anybody wants it, but because the circumstances which are being created will lead in that direction." To be sure, he admits, "some crazy guy [may try] to manipulate [the world] for a while, keep it stunted for a while. But the movement is in that direction."

One of the principal results of this movement, he says, will be the sense of community around the world. Already, he notes, Europe is becoming one entity with "no passports and a single currency." He sees North America and Latin America shortly following suit, with the inevitable further merging of these three entities into one. "Borders will be relics of the past," he says. "I think that's the trend. The closeness will come."

Is there a name for this trend? "The only name," he says, "is freedom of people as individuals. The more we can free a person, the more the world will [progress]. Any structure—social structure, economic structure—which restricts people will only delay the day." Both capitalism and communism, as now practiced, are far too restrictive for such freedom. "It's a race between the interpretation of [new] structures, economic and political, which release people."

One thing is certain: with the growth of telecommunications and travel, the centralization of such structures will disappear, and power will devolve to the local community level. "What you've got in Washington, I'll have in a tiny township with a population of 403—because I've got access to information. So you're not so big any more. You can't come and tell me, 'You don't know what's going on in tiny countries; you have to be in Washington to find out.' I say, 'You're crazy: I know everything!'"

As that difference between large and small communities fades, so too will the distinctions between what he calls "a big entrepreneur and a small entrepreneur." To Yunus, "every human being is important." At present, the world distinguishes between the "big" ones who "got the chance" and "displayed their importance," and the rest who never got a chance and ended up filling a slot.

"I think a human being is not created to fill anybody's slot," asserts Yunus. "He's a unique creation in the universe. He was never born before, however many million of years there were. And he will never be born in the future.

"That uniqueness cannot be torn away from me just because I need a job. I used to be a musician, I love music, but just because I have to have a job I become a bank clerk—that is an insult, that will disappear."

Central to these changes, he says, will be changing attitudes toward children. "I have tremendous faith in children," he says, because of what he calls "their absorptive capacity." Adults are "relics of the past" who "learn in certain ways and try to teach our children in the same way."

Already, he says, it is not uncommon for ten-year-olds to know more than fifty-year-olds. Yunus sees that in his own family, where his children already know more about computers than he does. "No matter what country you're in," he says, "the best people using computers are in high school."

What worries him, he says, is that "our failure as adults in providing the real challenges to the young people" will create "a lot of frustrations among them. They will not trust our systems—our systems of government, of business, our economic system." Alcohol, drugs, and violence, he feels, are symptoms of these frustrations. "Until we find the ethical structure that says, 'This is what we want, and we believe in it,' challenges will be lacking."

One of the challenges that Yunus and the Grameen Bank have thrown down within Bangladesh is a statement of the so-called "Sixteen Decisions" that Grameen borrowers are encouraged to uphold. One of them, which Yunus has described as "absolutely a radical idea," calls for the abolition of dowry, which is a social tradition so powerful in his country that it leads parents to look on the birth of girl children as "a disaster."

For Yunus, the tradition of dowry is part of a larger and even more divisive issue: the confusion of superstitions with religion. Although raised a Muslim, Yunus says that "formally I'm not a religious person." Informally, however, he thinks of himself as religious. "My religion is people," he says. Although he is convinced that "there is a God, there is a Creator," his overriding religious concern is the equality of all people, which, he feels, many religions talk about, and which ought to constitute "the real thread" binding different religions.

The problem, he says, is that "the bulk of religion is couched with superstitions. There's a religious framework, [which you] then put a lot of superstitions around and pass on as religion. That's where you start differing—because my superstitions and your superstitions don't agree." Islam, he says, is a case in point: the Indonesian Muslim, accustomed to pressing the hands together and bowing slightly as a form of greeting or respect, mightily offends the Bangladeshi Muslim, who associates that gesture with the Hindus.

Yet here, too, Yunus is hopeful for the future. "With the explosion of knowledge the way I'm seeing it, superstition just melts away—you cannot hold on to superstition."

For all his optimism, however, he remains cautious about the results of his successes as a lender—concerned that, as the poor in any society begin to rise toward wealth, they will lose the honesty and openness of their past and adopt the less truthful ways of the well-to-do.

"You have to hide a lot," Yunus explains, "when you're at the top. When you're at the bottom there's nothing to hide." The poor, he says, "remain truthful, very transparent, very honest people because they have not fooled around with anything. You find a lot of strength in people like that. They will wake you up in the middle of the night to give you back your money. But as you grow, you find out how not to give the money back. The biggest defaulters in Bangladesh are always the biggest people in Bangladesh."

Can such a loss of ethical character be prevented as poverty recedes and the poor become richer? Only if the "very painstaking process" used by the Grameen Bank and other lenders makes it difficult for borrowers to adopt "a different kind of system" from the honesty out of which they have come.

"This is your only hope," says Yunus, who notes that when microcredit lending is done properly it is "a very disciplined type of work."

That is a point often overlooked by the major banks—who, says Yunus, "keep insisting that Grameen's 'whole system is crazy, it will collapse.' "

"I say, 'Sixteen years, every day, we bank with all these people, and it has never happened. In 97 percent of the cases I'm right. So which system is better?' "

Kenneth Boulding

Peace as Well-Managed Conflict

*All the world's religions come out against
unmitigated selfishness. That's a
common ethos.*

During several hours of conversation on an August
afternoon, high Colorado clouds periodically
darken the sun shining on Kenneth Boulding's balcony in Bolder, Colorado. Each time they roll in, an electric-
powered awning automatically retracts—only to whir slowly
outward again to shade the area when the sun reappears.

For a man used to metaphors, that awning could well
symbolize his own career—always ready to shelter and pro-

tect the world from dangerous intensities, always willing to let the light stream in where needed, and never too rigid to adapt.

"I'm thinking of doing a book on the twenty-first century as the 'Age of Maturity,' " said Professor Boulding with a spry grin during a 1989 interview for this book. "We've been teenagers up to now. But when you get to be twenty-one, all growth is fat, so you have to be careful. But growth has to be spiritual, in a sense. And particularly in a world as divided as this, that isn't easy."

These, he said, are "just some ideas, but there's something in these metaphors and images that can capture the imagination."

Capturing the imagination has long been the special talent of this longtime member of the faculty of the University of Colorado. An English-born socioeconomist whose thirty-plus books have made him one of the most respected commentators on contemporary ideas, Boulding, who died in 1993, combined skillful scholarship with the deep convictions born of his Quaker faith. His work, spread across five decades, spans many disciplines: his 1985 book, *The World as a Total System,* is as wide ranging and comprehensive as its title suggests, while his recent work has focused more sharply on the nature of scientific inquiry.

With his Norwegian-born wife, Elise—a sociologist and author who is secretary-general of the International Peace Research Association and a recent nominee for the Nobel Peace Prize—he is widely credited with helping to launch the broad, citizen-based efforts for peace that developed in the 1950s. "They're the golden oldies of the peace movement," says Rev. William Sloane Coffin, the well-known anti-war activist. "I think they represent the kind of wisdom that only compassion can produce."

• • •

"Peace is well-managed conflict; war is a very poor form of conflict management."

If such aphorisms come naturally to the tongue of Kenneth Boulding, that's no accident: he helped invent the term "conflict resolution" in the 1950s and has worked hard since then to develop concepts that will bring peace to a fractured world.

"I've argued since the Second World War that we've had a great triangle of stable peace in Australia, Japan, and across North America to Finland. So you have eighteen countries that have no plans whatever to go to war with each other. Now it looks like it's just on the edge of expanding into the whole temperate zone."

The developing nations, he admits, are "another matter," given their poverty, population pressures, and relative political youth. While the superpower standoff stifled a number of would-be nationalistic feuds, the collapse of the Soviet Union has opened the way for new outbreaks of warfare.

Yet the real question, for Boulding, is why, after so many centuries of experience, warfare is still seen as accomplishing any useful goals. "Peace is something you have to learn, and how we encourage this human learning process is one of the great problems of the peace movement."

By contrast, he asserts, "conquest doesn't pay off very

well." It may produce the appearance of stability for several generations, until suddenly there arises "an astonishing collapse of legitimacy."

His prime piece of evidence: the former British Commonwealth. When he was a small boy in England, he says, "nobody questioned the British empire" except certain intellectuals on the radical fringe. "Yet even when I was at Oxford the whole thing began to crumble. It was very clear that it was a moral burden: Gandhi certainly made that clear. And it only took an entire generation to shuck off the whole thing. You see the same thing in the Soviet Union—it's just kind of left over from Queen Victoria, a nineteenth-century empire."

Another problem, he says, is what to do with "organizations that have to have an enemy in order to justify their budgets? How do you move the ethos of the military in a more creative direction? The bright people in the military recognize the jig's up—that the long-range missile and the nuclear weapon have destroyed the traditional military ethic."

What does he mean by *destroyed*? "This whole business of fighting and courage and combat and all that sort of stuff has gone down the drain," he explains. "For people who believe in deterrents, this is a hell of a situation for the military, isn't it? Because it's only useful as long as it's not being used. That's like having a football team that practices and practices and is never allowed to play"—except, he says, during such "little ritual wars" as the episodes in Libya, Grenada, and Panama that "give the military something to do."

The underlying problem, he says, is that "we haven't

got to the point in the nation-states where we recognize that national defense, in the traditional sense, has got to end." That doesn't mean an end of national security, he says, but simply an end of its "excessively military aspect."

The problem raised here, for Boulding, is part of a much larger and essentially ethical issue: how to change the fundamental systems of a society. It is clear, he says, that some social systems are more ethical than others—or, put another way, that "there are some ethical systems which get into more trouble than others." The collapse of Marxism, he says, "demonstrates the dangers of having a this-worldly religion. If you promise pie in the sky, that's hard to check up on. But if you promise pie for the grandchildren, and the grandchildren turn up and there's no pie, the whole thing's over. So we've had this great disillusionment with the Marxist ethos, because it just doesn't perform."

By contrast, he feels Islam is proving quite successful as an ethical system. Whatever the system, however, he feels it partakes of some fundamental values that it holds in common with other systems. "There is a lot of similarity in the great world religions," he notes, especially centering on the Golden Rule of loving your neighbor as yourself. "All the world's religions come out against unmitigated selfishness," he says. "So that's a common ethos."

Another point of common ground, he feels, is the "ethos of science" that has developed over the last four hundred years. He sees four ethical elements common to the scientific way of thinking. "One is a high value placed on curiosity—what's the world really like." Another is "a very high value on veracity—telling the truth. The thing that gets you run out of the scientific community is being caught at telling a lie—you falsify an experiment, that's the end of it."

A third, he says, "involves some sort of testing—the theory that all the images you have in your head are hypotheses, and they all represent approximations, so testing is a way of diminishing error." The fourth, he says, is "the abstention from threat," on the principle that "people should be persuaded by evidence and not by threat."

This ethos of science, he says, "corresponds very closely to the ethos of the common law." Curiosity, in law, involves finding out "what really happened, was it an accident or something else." Veracity involves telling "the whole truth and nothing but the truth." Testing, he says, surfaces in the act of cross-examination. As for the fourth point, he notes that "it's a fundamental principle that judges should be influenced only by the evidence presented in the court and not by threat."

Are those four points, then, common to all professions? Not entirely, he says. "The military have an ethic of their own—some qualities of courage and self-sacrifice—but they very much believe in threat."

In addition to these points, Boulding adds another to his code, which he describes as the need to "put a high value on variety." This, in his mind, is why the environmental movement is very important, since one of its great principles is a love of variety for its own sake. "If the blue whale is endangered, we feel worried about this, because we love the variety of the world. In some sense I feel about the Catholic church the way I feel about the blue whale: I don't think I'll be one, but I would feel diminished if it became extinct."

That threat of extinction, in fact, worries him greatly, not only among biological species but among what he calls "social species." Some years ago, he recalls flying for a weekend from South Africa to Kenya. "As we drove in from the airport I looked at Nairobi and said, 'Good Lord, we've landed in Wichita by mistake!' Skyscrapers and all—Nairobi looked very much like Wichita. I was struck by the creeping Wichitization of the world. Singapore looks like New York, Tokyo looks like New York, Berlin, Madrid. Where we stayed in the suburbs, it looked just like Dallas. The architecture is incredibly uniform—the era of the glass shoe boxes you find all over the world."

However much he worries about such uniformity, Boulding is aware that the diversity arising from a rich mix of cultures can breed its own problems. "I grew up in Liverpool," he recalls. "There was only one English Protestant family on the street where I grew up—all the others were Jewish or Irish. Every 12th of July we'd barricade the house and the Irish would riot outside it, and the next day we'd unbolt the door and clean the blood off the doorstep, and life would go on."

If that immersion in diversity illustrated for him the power of unresolved conflicts among nations, it also bred in him a respect for and acceptance of ethnic differences. "When I came to this country I felt at home immediately," he recalls. "This country was just Liverpool glorified: it was very easy for me to become an American."

In today's America, however, ethnic groups don't usually hold annual riots. So has the world's ethical tenor changed for the better since the days of his youth?

"There are ups and downs in these things," Boulding observes. "Certainly in the last forty years we've had an increase in crime and police and so forth. And drugs are much worse than they were in the days of opium." But he notes that "all societies have pathological subcultures. Whether ours is worse than the Middle Ages, I don't know. I figure that if things have got worse, they haven't got very much worse."

Among the factors contributing to improvement, he says, is "the development of the welfare state in the twentieth century"—which, while it has "had one or two wrong turns," has "on the whole" been "a very good thing." He also cites the "loosening up of class distinctions," the movement toward more universal education, and "the cleaning up of the cities." The latter trend he has seen in his own experience: the Liverpool of his youth, he says, was "an unspeakably filthy city," due in part to the kind of coal burned for heat. "I was in a fog in London where I couldn't see my feet," he recalls. "Now, that's air pollution!"

He also points to improvements in the growth of equality for women and the removal of racial barriers, two issues that, in his mind, are linked. "The genetic difference between men and women is very small," he says, "and the genetic difference between the races is even smaller. Genetics really undermines racism, because the genetic differences *within* the races are much greater than the differences *between* them. It's much the same with the sexes."

Fortunately, he says, "we've had this technical revolution in the household—about as great as in agriculture—and this has liberated women." As a result, "the presence of women in the labor force has nearly doubled in the last thirty years." While that trend has produced "some side effects, on child care and those sorts of things," in general he feels that "it has been a great change for the better."

Boulding remains concerned, however, about one notable characteristic of modern society, which he calls "a lack of communities of all ages."

"This is the great virtue of the church," he says, describing it as "almost the only community of all ages left. In the old days, young people—apprentices, farm boys—grew up in the presence of old people. Now we have this age segregation in high schools and colleges." The result, he says, is the development of "a youth culture that I think is disastrous." Why is that a problem? Because, he says with a chuckle, "the one thing we know about youth is that it doesn't have a future"—since young people, obviously, never remain young. What's important instead, he says, is the development of "an all-life culture"—although he admits that "the mobility of the family nowadays" makes it "much harder to sustain extended families."

On balance, however, Boulding sees himself as an optimist. Why? "Maybe it's just good digestion," he says with a grin. Then, more seriously, he notes that his optimism stems from an awareness of the permanence of truth and the ephemeral nature of error. "If you believe something that *isn't* so," he explains, "you're a little bit more likely to change it than if you believe something that *is* so. There's a little instability of error, and there really is a power of truth. This persists all the time: I think you can see this happening over history."

The point, he says, is that "people do, gradually, catch on." Turning to an example, he explains that "if I'm going in a plane, I don't want a pilot who believes in a flat earth"—since that belief would not be adequate to the task of flight or navigation. "It's a bit the same with these ethical things," he says. "There's an ethos that is inadequate. There's the same error problem here, you see: if you have an error in ethics, and if you have an ethos that 'isn't so,' as it were, then you're more likely to change it."

"You see this happening," he concludes. "That's what makes me an optimist."

James K. Baker

The Corporate Climate for Ethics

*We like to send the signal that everybody's
even, everybody's alike, everybody has the same
rights—no names in the parking lot.*

T here is no such thing as *'business* ethics.' "
Such a statement, coming from a former president (1990–1991) of the U. S. Chamber of Commerce, could well be a conversation stopper.

But James K. Baker doesn't stop there. "There's only
'ethics,' " he explains. "What you do over here is no different from what you do over there. Let's not think that you've

got to adhere to one standard at home and another standard at work. There's only one thing."

As chairman and CEO of Arvin Industries, a Fortune 500 manufacturer located in Columbus, Indiana, most of Baker's thinking on the subject has been done in the context of corporate life and has grown straight up from the grassroots ethos of middle America, where he is widely admired for his ethical standards. A graduate of DePauw University in nearby Greencastle, Baker admits that he still looks for "Midwestern" values when he recruits for Arvin. Yet his activities carry him far beyond his Midwestern roots and into a global context: Arvin, a major manufacturer of automotive parts, has plants in seventeen countries and employs some 5,500 people overseas.

That global vision, however, has not disconnected him from his community roots. "Among all the business leaders I know," says Edward Donley, chairman of the Executive Committee of Air Products and Chemicals, Inc., in Allentown, Pennsylvania, "he's one of the most committed to public service and doing things for the community."

"I think the amount of time and effort that he puts into the needs of this community have stirred everybody else up to a greater actual participation," says J. Irwin Miller, former chairman of Cummins Engine Company, also located in Columbus. "He's a model of what a citizen ought to be."

Peter Likins, president of Lehigh University, also gives him high marks. Both men are members of the Business–Higher Education Forum, an organization of corporate leaders and university presidents. Likins notes that Baker has been "especially effective from the perspective of the academics in demonstrating real compassion, and integrity, and concern, and sensitivity, while at the same time bringing the businessman's point of view to the dialogue."

•   •   •

Ask James K. Baker where his interest in ethics comes from, and the lean, quiet-spoken tennis player traces it to a piece of fourth-class mail that arrived in 1978 inviting him to an ethics conference at Bentley College in Waltham, Massachusetts.

At the conference, sitting on a panel with a CEO whose corporation had one of the oldest codes of ethics in the nation, he was impressed by the man's eloquence. Two weeks later, he recollects, "his company's name popped up in the *Wall Street Journal*" when half a dozen of its officials had been indicted for a seven-million-dollar problem in Europe.

"Here was a guy whose whole intent was in being ethical," says Baker, recalling the experience during an extended interview in Indianapolis. "And I thought, 'There's something missing—what is it?' " That missing ingredient, he finally concluded, was "the personal trust and personal relationship between two people."

"Big companies don't think about that very much," he says. "But a big company is simply a combination of lots of two-people relationships."

That same year Baker's company, Arvin Industries, began a reporting system that encouraged one-on-one communication between employees and their immediate superiors. Baker saw how well the system worked one day when the company's chief purchasing agent came to his boss. He wanted to discuss an all-expenses-paid golfing Florida vacation he had been offered with a group of executives whose company supplied steel to Arvin. The purchasing agent and his boss, recalls Baker, "worked out that he would take a week's vacation, he'd pay his own hotel expense, and he would allow them to buy only one meal a day for him. It was a good, ethical solution to what could have been a breach of what we thought were good ethical standards. I was encouraged that the one-on-one kind of relationship—respect, trust—was the right way to promulgate good ethics."

A different sort of case arose in 1968 when Baker, at age thirty-seven, had just been made executive vice president. Reporting to him was a man twenty years his senior, for whom Baker had once worked. "He came to me and said, 'Would it be all right if we sent airline tickets to this purchasing agent in Philadelphia who works for the government? He and his wife want to go to his daughter's college graduation in California.' "

Though the law made it illegal for the purchasing agent to accept such a gift, it was not yet illegal (as it would become a few years later under the Foreign Corrupt Practices Act) for Arvin to offer it. Furthermore, the Arvin executive felt that future government orders of Arvin products would be highly dependent upon his answer.

"My response was one of great impatience," says Baker, who notes that he might have more patience today. "I went to my boss within one or two hours and said that I felt that this was cause for dismissal: if he even *considered* that there was a likelihood for approval, there was something wrong, and his standards were not like the rest of ours."

The next day, Baker recalls, the Arvin employee was fired.

Today, he notes, "we have built into our system a little more leniency, in that if you've got an ethical dilemma you don't get hit over the head quite as hard as I hit him. But I was kind of an impatient young man, and I just couldn't believe what I'd just heard."

The point, says Baker, is that ethical behavior in business includes "everything you do." The salesman who adds one hundred miles to his mileage on an expense account "has to be caught," says Baker, and his boss has to let him know that such fudging is not acceptable. "The guy who goes for that extra hundred miles on the expense report—twenty years later he may go for something that's really bad."

For Baker, that sense of ethics also extends into sexual morality, particularly regarding extramarital relationships. "Here's a case where we have higher standards for officers than we have for everybody else. I still believe that the vows of a marriage are something to be respected by two people—and if they're not, most others tend not to respect the individuals." The point, he says, is that an officer engaged in an extramarital affair may be so diminished in respect—especially in rural, conservative Indiana—that he will no longer be able to lead others.

How does a company promote a high standard of ethics? The answer, for Baker, does not lie in making lots of rules. "There's not a policeman standing behind every post," he says. Neither a company nor a nation can "design enough regulations to catch all of the temptations, all of the areas of unethical behavior. So you're just going to have to create an environment that promotes good, sound ethical behavior."

That environment, he says, is set by the senior officers. "When I came to the company, at twenty-five or twenty-six years old, I had a great deal of respect for all of the leaders of the company, because of the kind of gentlemen they were. And I think that's something to be remembered—that young people really do sense the tone in a company. They really do know if there are some corners being cut."

"And let me tell you how you cut corners. If I drive in in the morning—our working hours are 8 to 5—having had a second or a third cup of coffee, and I arrive at 10 minutes after 8 and park in the very front of the parking lot, with a sign that says, 'Mr. Baker'—they don't like that. That's not ethical. That sends the wrong signal. We like to send the signal that everybody's even, everybody's alike, everybody has the same rights—no names in the parking lot.

"I remember in 1980 a union in Columbus had a little dispute with management, and they carried a few signs around, and my name was on a few of them. And one of those signs said, 'Is he really worth six of us?' because my salary was six times what their average pay was.

"I don't apologize for that. I do have a different level of responsibility. I'm well trained for the job and the level of responsibility I have. But when it comes to human rights within our company, I'm equal to them, they're equal to me. You send out so many signals by treating yourself special—with big black limousines and parking places and executive washrooms and special stationery and so on. And I think that tends to—instead of increase the respect, which in some sense you think it's doing—it does just the opposite."

Baker is concerned, however, that many corporate CEO's don't see it that way. Just as society's ethical standards have lowered, he says, so CEO standards have also lowered. He traces the problem to increased pressure, and to the belief that "making big bucks" is always best for the shareholders.

"I think that's very different from saying, 'What's right for the shareholders? What's right for this company? What's right for employees?' That's not the yardstick, unfortunately."

Baker recalls that "a very fine businessman" once looked at his year-end statement and commented, " 'You have no idea how to avoid taxes.' " Some companies, he points out, "go to great lengths to avoid taxes, with all kinds of tax havens and dummy corporations and Carribbean offices. This is not our game. We pay our fair share of taxes because we think, being a good citizen, that we should do so."

That attempt to beat the regulations concerns him greatly, he says. "It's not the lawyers' fault, it's not the accountants' fault, it's not the regulators' fault. It's the fault of the business leaders. We seem to try to find holes in the law. Even if we know the law is right and hits the nail on the head, we still wonder if we can't beat it."

If he could do one thing for the nation, he says, he would try to "convince every CEO in this country that it is strictly up to them to set the tone of ethics in their company. I think they're listening to their lawyers. And I don't want to blame their lawyers. But the lawyers are saying, 'Hey, we didn't violate any laws: We're ethical.' "

Recently, discussing a possible deal with a Japanese businessman, Baker recalls that he was "really set back" on his heels when the man said, in essence, " 'We put personal relations first, financial issues second, and legal issues last. You Americans have it just in the opposite order.' "

Is there, then, a set of standards that Americans, Japanese, and others around the world could agree to—a kind of universal code of ethics?

Admitting that it's "a tough question," Baker returns to his emphasis on "trust and respect between two people, no matter how large the organization." Out of that, he says, grows the first point he would place on his code: that "if you're working for me, I want you first of all to know that you have the right to differ with me on anything that I say.

"Now, I hope you'll do it in the confines of my office or yours, so that we can discuss it," he adds. "But if I give you some marching orders, and you feel there's an unethical tone to them, you have the right to pop up and say, 'Jim, stop—let's talk about this a minute.' I think the right to differ with authority is at the heart of an ethical environment."

A related point, he says, has to do with establishing an environment in which there is "more pleasure in intelligent dissent than in passive agreement. Almost any organization is going to be better off if they have that environment. And if that carries throughout the organization, ethics will not be something on which there can be no intelligent dissent."

He feels, however, that companies make a mistake by

placing too much emphasis on codes of ethics. Such codes, he says, "typically make the reader believe that if they follow that one page or those twelve pages they're going to be ethical."

The problem, he says, is that sound ethical behavior is far beyond mere adherence to the law. "It's not just signing the year-end statement that I have read the code and I agree with it and I have adhered to it this past year. That's where you start, not where you end. That gives a false signal to people. That's just the baseline. We have a standard much higher than that. People need to have support to encourage them to operate beyond conventional ethics."

In addition, he says, corporations need to understand that ethics is a long-term commitment, and they need to keep an eye on their future reputations. "A company has its own history. People will know if I guided this company into Europe in a very ethical way, even though I was very opportunistic and I wanted to do it with great dispatch. They'll know whether I bent any rules or rounded any corners. But they'll know it best five years from now."

Finally, Baker returns to the need for trust. "I've been in very quiet rooms with only one other person who had a great deal of power, and I've shaken hands with the person on a deal, only to have it broken."

"With that shake of hands went an exchange of trust. To me, if that is absent, then I really do believe that business can grind to a halt. Little by little, if we let that trust go out of our personal dealings with one another, then I think the system really begins to have trouble."

Newton Minow

Rights, Responsibilities, and Television

*We've gotten to the point where everybody's got
a right and nobody's got a responsibility. I
suppose that's the ultimate result of our society
being afraid to distinguish between
wrong and right.*

On May 9, 1961, a young lawyer used three words
that lodged permanently in the public discourse
about American television. Speaking as President
Kennedy's newly appointed chairman of the Federal Communications Commission (FCC), Newton Minow blasted
the National Association of Broadcasters for allowing commercial television to become "a vast wasteland."

Thirty years later, in a speech before the Gannett Foundation Media Center at Columbia University that reexamined the wasteland, he found it even vaster. "In 1961, I worried that my children would not benefit much from television," he said, "but in 1991 I worry that my grandchildren will actually be harmed by it." Overall, he gave television "an A+ for technology, but only a C for using that technology to serve human and humane goals."

In the intervening years, that focus on humane goals has characterized Minow's life. Shortly after his FCC appointment, he openly distanced himself from any potential conflict of interest by declaring that "I'm not interested in being reappointed, and I don't want a job in the industry." Serving for only two years, he has since been chairman of the Public Broadcasting Service, chairman of the Rand Corporation, and twice cochair of the televised debates between presidential candidates. Proud of his Jewish heritage—though noting that "I'm not especially observant"—he has been chairman of the board of overseers of the Jewish Theological Seminary and remains the sole Jewish trustee of Notre Dame University.

A trustee of Northwestern University and chairman of the board of the Carnegie Corporation, he is a director of the Public-Service Television Project for the American Academy of Arts and Sciences, which seeks to "define a contemporary public-interests standard for television and promote discussion of a national communications policy for the twenty-first century." An attorney with Sidley & Austin, he has three grown daughters and lives with his wife, Jo, in Chicago.

•   •   •

From the fifty-fifth floor of his Chicago law firm's offices, Newton Minow surveys a downtown area that has changed dramatically during his lifetime—from glamorous vitality through grimy neglect and finally back to a new vibrancy. Through his decades of public service and private practice here and in Washington, Minow has had equal opportunity to survey the vicissitudes of human experience. Standing out as a constant in all that change: the importance of an ethical sense.

"As I've gotten older," says Minow during a ninety-minute interview over iced tea in one of his firm's conference rooms, "I've become less and less partisan in my view. I don't think the issues break down between Democrats and Republicans, between liberals and conservatives, between business and labor. I think what is at stake here is [the distinction between] right and wrong."

It is that distinction, or rather the lack of it, that gives him greatest concern. "The dominant characteristic, I'm afraid, of our current society [is] an unwillingness to confront what we regard as evil, or wrong, and say so. We have become unwilling to say, 'This is right and this is wrong.' "

Instead, he says, we have developed a taste for saying, " 'Who am I to tell you what's right or wrong? Why should I impose my views on you?' "

The result, he says, is a society which teaches ethics even while it insists that it isn't. "When you've got the distribution of condoms in schools, what you've really done is to teach ethics in schools, but redefine what you mean by ethics."

"I think our society has to be willing to say certain values are treasured and certain activities are unacceptable. You have to start with that. And when you tell me, 'It may be right or wrong for you, but it's not for me,' I'm going to say, 'There are some things that are universally applicable to every one of us.' "

What are those things? Asked to list his candidates for a global code of values, Minow responds succinctly. "I'm not sure we've improved much over the Ten Commandments," he says. "After thousands of years those universal truths have as much validity now as they did then."

These commandments, found in the Old Testament of Christianity and in the Torah of Minow's Jewish upbringing, focus both on humanity's relation to God and on moral laws governing human interrelations. The last six commandments, in fact, form one of the most concise ethical codes ever articulated: honor your father and mother, and do not kill, commit adultery, steal, bear false witness, or covet.

"Most of the Ten Commandments, last time I read them, are in the negative," says Minow. "You shouldn't do this, you shouldn't do that, this is forbidden, that's a no-no, and so on." That, he says, is all to the good—a needed counterbalance in a society that has put far too much emphasis on *rights* and far too little on *responsibilities*.

That imbalance of rights and responsibilities came home to Minow when he and his wife went to China in the 1970s, long before it was popular for Americans to do so. "When you go to a totally different culture," he says, "it forces you to examine ideas that you have taken for granted. By the force of comparison you learn more about your own country than the country you visit."

As a lawyer, he was particularly interested in comparing attitudes toward law. "The Chinese start with the premise that the law exists to protect the state from the individual," he says. In the West, by contrast, "we start with the premise that the law exists to protect the individual from the state."

Beginning at opposite poles, he says, both societies "went bananas to excess in opposite directions." In China, where responsibility to the community was the driving force, "the individual ended up in effect being a slave of the state." Meanwhile, in a United States dominated by concern over individual rights, "people were imprisoned in their homes and apartments because they were afraid of crime on the streets. We had a society that seemed more concerned about the rights of the criminal than the rights of the victim."

Now, he says, "both societies are in the process, like a pendulum, of coming back toward a more centered view." While he certainly does not advocate a Chinese-style dismissal of rights, he insists that the United States needs to move strongly toward the side of responsibility. "I believe the basic reason we got off the track was that rights became more important than responsibilities, that individuals became more important than community interests. We've gotten to the point where everybody's got a right and nobody's got a responsibility. I suppose that's the ultimate result of our society being afraid to distinguish between wrong and right."

Even in his own profession, Minow sees a lack of ability to distinguish right from wrong. "My profession is in very bad standing with the public right now," he says, citing the number of lawyers involved in Watergate and the steady

First Amendment rights whenever the editor or publisher decides not to publish a book."

The second problem with such arguments, says Minow, is that the invocation of First Amendment rights is usually thought of as "the end of the subject, when it really is the beginning." Minow points out that if an individual criticized for socially offensive speech or behavior responds by saying, " 'I'm invoking my First Amendment rights,' the correct answer to that is: 'Well, you have a right to say something and so do I. And I have as much of a right to say I think you're wrong.' "

Supreme Court Justice Potter Stewart, Minow recalls, "said it all in one phrase: just because you have the right to do something, or say something, does not make it the right thing to do."

What, then, is the relation between law and ethics? "Law is the end result of an ethical consensus in a community," says Minow, "which is then articulated and enforced. Law reflects what is prohibited and what is not." Ethics, by contrast, reflects "a higher standard than law" that has not yet been fully accepted by the community to the point that it can be written into law and enforced.

Why is the nation in such confusion over the rights-and-responsibility issue? In part, Minow says, because we are not educating the next generations in our core values. He notes that the three standard vehicles for moral education—home, family, and school—are struggling. To these, however, he adds a fourth: television.

"If you study the numbers as I do," he says, "a child now spends more time with the television set than with the

186

teacher. In many homes, a child spends more time with the TV set than with the parent." That in itself may not be bad, given that television is "the most important educational institution in America." Unfortunately, he feels, it has been so misused that "in many ways [it] has contributed to the demise of ethical standards and values in our country."

The solution, he is quick to point out, does not lie in censorship. As a nation, he says, "we believe, I think correctly, in free expression and the First Amendment. We do not believe that anyone, particularly the government, should censor radio or television."

But in a free market, producers constantly seek the originality that may give their programs a competitive edge. So "the Hollywood creative community is always pushing the envelope farther and farther towards the edge of what's acceptable." One result, he says, is that sex has become "a constant television preoccupation," presented in a context in which "you don't have to be mature adults, you don't have to be married."

Another result is excessive violence, "where we see, over and over again, the solution to a problem coming at the point of a gun, or a beating, or whatever. You read about one of these eleven-year-old kids shooting somebody—I'm not saying television caused the child to do it, but certainly television did not discourage it. I think it's a terrible waste of this powerful medium to fill it as we are, over and over again, with a shot from a gun. I think there are great moral issues involved."

But can television become a moral force? Minow feels certain that it can. He points to research showing that, when a socially desirable concept is woven into popular weekly programs, it begins to affect viewers positively. Example: when a television character asks "Who's the designated driver?" during a sitcom drinking scene, that bit of dialogue can help make such a concept socially acceptable. Similarly, television can be used to help reduce bad habits: as FCC chairman, Minow launched the prohibition of smoking commercials, which remains in effect today.

But given that so much of American television is privately owned and run for profit, can "moral" television ever make money? "That's the interesting thing," he says. "People in the television business seem to think that you need to have a lot of violence, a lot of sex. Yet the programs that seem to be the most popular, the most enduring, are not those." He points to "The Cosby Show," which during its run held the top-rated slot on television and "taught a great lesson to the American people" about a black family with high standards and lots of "caring for each other."

In an effort to understand where the medium is headed, Minow is currently writing a book about the future of television. Around the turn of the century, he says, television and computers will be interconnected in a five hundred-channel environment. As viewers, he says, we will no longer "watch programs when the broadcaster sends them to us, but rather when we want to see them." Also disappearing from the map: video stores, which will be replaced by direct access from the home computer to a video library.

"I think there's a technological revolution about to occur before our eyes," he says. "What *we're* wrestling with is, what is the role, if any, of the government in that kind of environment? Do you leave the marketplace to take care of itself?" While he doesn't believe government should stay out altogether, he's unclear how it should be involved.

He does see room for intervention, however, to help resolve the "terrible ethical problem" involving television and electoral politics. The average U. S. Senator, he says, has "got to raise something like $20,000 each and every week he's in office, basically to buy TV time" for reelection. The result, he notes, is that special-interest funding dominates Congress, a problem that could be solved if television time were made available to candidates in ways other than through purchase.

He also worries that, in a five hundred-channel environment, there will so much diversity that there will be few common points of interest to unite the nation. He recalls that French President Charles De Gaulle once asked how you could ever unite a nation that has 264 kinds of cheese. For the United States, says Minow, "the question's going to be, 'How can you unite a nation that has five hundred television channels?' We're going to be missing that common shared experience."

For all his concerns, however, Minow remains optimistic about the ethical future. "We've become afraid, somehow, of values," he says. "We now, I hope, are coming back."

John W. Gardner

Creating Community in a Pluralistic World

People of radically differing beliefs have found
it possible to live peacefully with one another.
They've found some kind of common ground.
They've found ways to work in the same offices,
to obey the same traffic signals.

When John W. Gardner travels, he jokes that he's the kind of person who leaves things behind—his notebooks, his pens, his briefcase. Addressing a small meeting in New York shortly before this interview, he had to borrow a friend's glasses—he'd mislaid his own—to read his notes.

Those who know him, however, agree that he's best at leaving behind a breathtaking array of ideas and institutions for the benefit of humanity. Among them: Common Cause, the well-known citizens' lobby he founded in 1970, and Independent Sector, a coalition of nonprofit organizations, corporations, and foundations interested in philanthropy and volunteerism that he cofounded in 1980.

"He's one of the few authentic wisemen I know," says Harlan Cleveland, former ambassador to NATO and former dean of the Hubert H. Humphrey Institute of Public Affairs at the University of Minnesota. "If there were a role of philosopher laureate—that's what he really is in our society."

Educated in psychology at Stanford University and the University of California, Gardner has been president of the Carnegie Corporation and the Carnegie Foundation for the Advancement of Teaching; secretary of Health, Education, and Welfare under Lyndon Johnson; chairman of the National Urban Coalition; and a member of various task forces and commissions under presidents Kennedy, Johnson, Carter, and Reagan. His seven books include *Excellence, Self-Renewal,* and *The Recovery of Confidence.* A native Californian, he is currently the Miriam and Peter Haas Professor of Public Service at Stanford.

"He's one of my hero figures," admits Andrew Heiskell, former chief executive officer of Time, Inc., and former chairman of the President's Committee on the Arts and the Humanities. Having watched Gardner chair meetings of sometimes contentious groups, he notes that "he has a very sensitive ear to various claimants—he knows how to respond to them and gather them into the fold."

● ● ●

In a lifetime of public service and private thought, John W. Gardner has tackled the tough subjects—the nature of excellence, the quest for self-renewal, the need for confidence. Now, with the completion of his latest book, *On Leadership*, he's focusing on the concept of community: what produces it, what keeps it together, why it matters.

But the subject behind these subjects, he says, is the question of ethics and values, a topic he says he's "been circling around for thirty years." Leadership, community, and ethics are all interwoven, he observes, because "it's very hard to lead a noncommunity. It's very hard to lead a group of people who have no consensus with respect to values. I don't mean unity, I mean some common ground that you can reach for."

Is there, then, a common core of values shared by people around the world—a kind of global ethic? The question, put to him over a noisy hotel breakfast during a visit to New York, elicits a boyish grin, a thought-gathering pause, and an answer resonant with decades of insight.

"I think this is a long, slow exploration to discover common ground," he begins. Noting that he is "not pessimistic," he says that "there is already some common ground, and I believe that we can find even more."

How do you find it? Using the ocean as a metaphor, he points out that "some values with respect to the meaning of life and the universe and one's religious faith are so deep that you can't compromise them. We can't ask people to compromise their beliefs in their God." On the other extreme, however, "we don't want to deal with the whitecaps on the surface," where the mere mannerisms of a society are often mistaken for real values.

But in the "middle depth," he observes, there's "a band of values" that many people can agree on. Although rooted in religious traditions, they are essentially secular values—a distinction Gardner emphasizes. "When you talk secular values," he says, "some religious thinkers are scornful. 'Those aren't the deepest things!' they say. Maybe they're not. But they're where you can establish some common ground—and where in fact humanity has established its common ground from the beginning."

What, then, are the common global values—values upon which most people in most cultures would agree? Gardner ticks them off slowly, thoughtfully.

• *Justice.* "I consider that probably the Number One candidate for your common ground," he says. "Fair play, or some word for even-handedness." That concept, he says, appears throughout the ages as a defining feature of societies that work.

• *Liberty.* This idea also has a long history, he notes, making it much broader than the modern American meanings. "Just ask, 'What did it mean in the ancient world? What did it mean in different cultures?' You discover that very early the concept of degrees of freedom of my action—as against excessive constraints on my action by a tyrant or by military conquerors—emerged. People knew when they were subjugated. And by and large people preferred not being subjugated by a military conqueror to being subjugated. They preferred not being slaves to being slaves. So freedom is again very deep—and, if we don't get too sophisticated about it too soon, a widely held value."

• *Equality of opportunity.* Gardner doesn't especially like the phrase, but uses it as a shorthand for "the release of human possibilities, the things in you that can come out regardless of your station, regardless of your past." He also recognizes that many people think of equality of opportunity as part of justice.

"The reason I would separate it out is that there were many rich concepts of justice current in the world for a long time before the concept of equality of opportunity, which somehow developed in the breakup of things at the time of the Renaissance, the industrial revolution, and then of course particularly in the United States."

The concept flourished in America, he notes, not because Americans are "any better" than other people, but because "we walked away from the ancient web of things that held human possibilities in check. And all kinds of people were free to develop."

• *The dignity of the individual.* By that, Gardner means "you don't demean people." This value, he feels, has deeply religious roots, stemming from "the belief that everyone has a soul." When the Spanish conquistadors came to the New World, he says, "they were not essentially any kindlier than we were. But they were accompanied by priests who felt very strongly that the native peoples had immortal souls, and they treated them substantially better as a result."

• *Tolerance.* "If you're serious about values, then you have to add tolerance very early—*very* early. Because you have to have constraints. The more you say, 'Values are important,' the more you have to say, 'There are limits to which you can impose your values on me.'

"And that is so hard to sustain! It's one of the toughest things in religion. I've watched many people go through this process of becoming more deeply religious. It's very hard for them to maintain a level of tolerance. In a way, that's almost natural: if you really believe that your immortal soul is in danger if you hold certain beliefs, it's natural for you to pull away from those who hold those dreadful beliefs."

Distinguishing between two sorts of tolerance, Gardner notes that what is needed is not "the tolerance that says, 'I know the truth, but I'm going to put up with this fellow who doesn't.' " Needed instead, he says, is the tolerance that says, " 'I may not know the whole truth. I may not know how God intended to communicate with all his children, and I better keep a little reserve of tolerance.' "

Is it possible, given such a menu of values, to find a common ground on which humanity can act? "Let me say some encouraging things," says Gardner. In many American cities, he observes, "a great many people of radically differing beliefs have found it possible to live peacefully with one another. They've found some kind of common ground. Maybe the secret is in not pushing it too far and insisting on the common ground. But they've found ways to work in the same offices, to obey the same traffic signals. It goes on all the time. Nations trade peaceably with one another.

So you have to start out saying, 'There's a capacity for accommodation here that we may not have fully used.' "

Gardner's long experience in knitting together groups of unlikely individuals—in government and nonprofit groups, as well as in Common Cause and Independent Sector—have convinced him that "there are some mechanisms that work" to create accommodation in social groups. "There is something in the human system that is probably a relic of the first urban complexes back in Mesopotamia, or the city of Ur, or wherever it was, that make life possible," he says.

His chairmanship of the National Urban Coalition in the late 1960s proved to him the value of seeking that common ground. The coalition, he notes, was "an absolutely extraordinary collection of leaders—maybe the most extraordinary we've ever had in the private sector. Men like Henry Ford and David Rockefeller, George Meany and Walter Reuther (who couldn't stand one another), Mayor Lindsey and Mayor Daly (who couldn't stand one another), the leading minority figures of the day, and so forth."

"It became apparent at once that there was no way of getting them to agree on many things. The task was to find things that they could agree on, things about which they would all say, 'Yes, this we can build on.' And if we could find those, we could find the area in which we operated, and set the rest aside."

The result was the formation of a kind of community, which, as he says, is "absolutely critical" for the establishment of ethics. "Common ground emerges when a community is formed," he says. "In fact, in my judgment, the values are generated out of face-to-face dealing in the family, the school, the church."

The need for today, he says, is for a definition of community that involves "what I call wholeness incorporating diversity." Gardner is convinced that the day of the homogeneous community, with its emphasis on wholeness rather than diversity, is gone. "It's too vulnerable," he says, noting that "it can only preserve its homogeneity by practices we don't approve of."

"The nostalgic feeling about the old traditional community, which is of course in our minds the great seedbed of values, is hopelessly anachronistic," he explains. "You can't bring it back, and if you brought it back it would be hopelessly inappropriate. We have to be heterogeneous and have to live with the pluralistic."

He especially faults "the resistance to change" so characteristic of many traditional communities. Today, he says, "you not only have to have a community that accommodates change but one that seeks change." He also worries that communities fail to move forward because of "the existence of the long-standing tradition." Community traditions are necessary, he says, but "today you have to go out and create your traditions."

One thing is sure: the outward appearance of "community" does not guarantee the inner spirit of communal effort. His studies of church congregations, for example, convinced him that there were "enormous differences in whether they were in fact 'communities.' Some of them have simply gained diversity, without discovering how to create a wholeness within which that diversity can live."

Yet building such wholeness is essential. "I almost see that as the task for our generation. How do you recreate some measure of wholeness of a community, respecting the inevitable diversity tracing from our religious differences, our ethnic differences, and so forth? That's true whether you're talking about Los Angeles, or Lebanon, or wherever."

In Gardner's mind, building community values and creating leaders are inseparable. "You want your network of leaders—and I think of leaders as running down through all levels and segments of the system—to affirm the values. And you want them to renew the values. Martin Luther King, affirming values that we weren't being true to, was doing just as much the leader's job as a very conventional mainstream leader. Every great dissenter who reminds us of things we've forgotten or neglected is also a leader."

In these terms, then, is the United States being well led?

"You mean at the top?" he says, musing for a moment on the question. "No, I don't think we are. Partly because I think campaign finance patterns have corrupted the electoral process, and partly because we need a much healthier substratum of leaders down the line before we can get great leadership at the top."

But leadership down the line requires a consensus, a common purpose and a common ground of values. "You see it in a war, or in anything that creates common purpose: you get greater leaders."

FIVE

Literature and Journalism
Listening to More Voices

*Maybe now we are listening to more voices
because it's a multiverse society, a more
open society.*

—Sergio Muñoz

Nien Cheng

Old Values in a New China

*One should basically know what is right and
what is wrong—and, when you know that, be
courageous enough to stand for what is right.*

s China and the West dance gingerly toward a
rapprochement, the ghost of the 1989 Tiananmen Square crackdown still hovers over the relationship. And while there are hints of new understandings,
China remains an enigma to outsiders. What are China's
fundamental values? Where will they lead the nation in the
twenty-first century?

Nien Cheng is uniquely suited to address such questions. Author of the highly acclaimed *Life and Death in Shanghai,* she was born in Peking, where her father was a vice minister in the navy. In 1935, while studying at the London School of Economics, she met her husband, Kang-chi Cheng. After Mao Tse-tung's communist victory in 1949, her husband was general manager of Shell in Shanghai—the only multinational oil company to remain in China under the new regime—until his death in 1957. Because he had been an official in Chiang Kai-shek's regime, however, the Red Guards ransacked her home in 1966, plunging her into six-and-a-half years of solitary confinement and brutal torture at the hands of the communists. After Mao's death in 1976, Cheng emmigrated to Ottawa, Canada, later moving to Washington, D.C., where she still lives.

She is a consummate "insider"—educated in Confucian schools, raised in a culture so traditional that her mother's marriage was arranged, and hired by Shell Oil after her husband's death to help negotiate the complexities of Chinese social and governmental relations. Yet she brings an outsider's freshness and perspective from her education in England, her conversion to Christianity, and her soul-searching years in prison. A slight, alert, and altogether gracious woman, she has been much in demand on the campus lecture circuit, where her compelling message of inner strength in the face of external adversity has made deep impressions on student audiences.

● ● ●

"There is a moral crisis in China."

In that quiet-spoken phrase, Nien Cheng cuts to the pith of the issues facing modern China. The words are not lightly spoken: even in the serene morning sunlight of her Washington condominium, one senses the decades of deep thought and wrenching experience behind her assertion.

It is not that she ignores the other issues—economic, political, military, social—facing China as it inches toward modernity. A frequent lecturer on these subjects, with a second book currently in progress, she keeps herself well versed on the latest details. But again and again in the course of a wide-ranging two-hour interview, she turns to the underlying values of Chinese society as a way of explaining its history and assessing its future.

"We behave according to the way we think," says Cheng in her flawless English. Of paramount interest, then, is the question of why today's Chinese think as they do, which, for her, is an essentially moral question.

The answers lead her back to the communist dictatorship of Mao Tse-tung, under whom she suffered such anguish and whose thought she came to understand so well. Chairman Mao, she says, "tried to destroy the old and impose the new. He failed utterly to impose the new, but he succeeded to a certain extent in destroying the old."

Result: the Chinese, isolated for so long from the rest of the world and yet torn from the moral moorings of their own traditions, are drifting uncomfortably into the twenty-first century.

"The Chinese people, basically, are rather arrogant," says Cheng. "Due to ignorance, they know only their own history." Building on that long-standing isolationism, the communist leaders were somewhat successful in persuading the people that they were keeping pace, economically and socially, with the rest of the world—a success that depended on keeping news of the outside world from penetrating China.

With the growth of communications technology, however, that penetration was inevitable. With it came a recognition of the economic standards enjoyed by the non-communist world.

"I think the Chinese have been demoralized," she says, "because of the sudden shock of realizing that they were so poor, so backward."

In the end, the communists, whom Cheng now considers to be thoroughly discredited in the eyes of most Chinese, failed to stem the flow of information. They were more successful, however, in suppressing China's traditional teachings, especially those of Confucius, whose philosophies have echoed throughout the Orient for two thousand years.

Yet while they officially replaced his teachings with what she calls the "political indoctrination and brainwashing" of Marx and Mao, the communists never succeeded in reaching the depth of the entrenched values growing out of those teachings. Even today, says Cheng, those values are "so absorbed into people's daily life and customs and habits that the people are not aware that they are behaving according to Confucius."

Today, she says, "nobody in China would openly believe in Confucius. He would be considered a diehard, out of touch with reality—though his behavior may be guided unconsciously by Confucius' teachings."

What are those teachings? Like most of her generation, Cheng, who was brought up in "the Confucian way," knows them well.

"When I was six years old, I went to school," she recalls. "I was so nervous, and the teacher led me by my hand into another room where there was a big painting, a scroll of Confucius. I had to kneel down and knock my head on the ground three times—meaning that from now on I must abide by the teachings of Confucius."

Foremost among those teachings, she says, is the concept that "you have to be responsible for your behavior—for everything that you do—or take the consequences."

That sense of responsibility, she says, is still a central force in Chinese society today. Most notably, it underlies the renowned Chinese work ethic, which is as visible among immigrants as it is at home.

"I read that the Russians have huge amounts of potatoes rotting in the field because they don't have trucks," says Cheng, turning for comparison to the northern neighbor so frequently looked to as the standard by the early Chinese communists. "Now, that would never happen in China, because the Chinese peasants don't depend on trucks. They will carry [the crop themselves] if they can make some money—they will do it any way they can."

The difference, she says, lies in the concept of hard work as "something to be proud of," rather than "something that you bargain over so that you work as little as possible." To be "the first to work hard, to work more, to work fifteen hours a day" is a characteristic that can be traced straight back to Confucius.

Cheng also points to a second aspect of Confucian

teaching: the well authenticated reluctance of the Chinese, even those of considerable wealth, to give to charitable causes. This reluctance, she feels, is another manifestation of the sense of responsibility—in that "a man must look after himself" rather than rely on contributions from others.

Even if they are "hard up," she says, many Chinese would not turn to charity or to the government for welfare. So powerful is this reticence, says Cheng, that it still operates strongly among otherwise Americanized Chinese immigrants in the United States. She recalls a recent conversation with a friend in Washington who told of paying for a blood test and never making any claim for reimbursement—even though she was entitled to government medical insurance.

"This is Confucius' teaching," says Cheng. "You must take care of yourself. To rely on others is a great shame."

Noting that this philosophy is "so contrary to socialist principles," Cheng points implicitly to one of the great difficulties the communists had in preaching the Marxist thesis of "to each according to his wants." At bottom, she says, the Confucian-taught Chinese "despise those who rely on the government."

That point helps explain a third trait of Confucianism: the dominance of the group over the individual. Building on this point, the Marxists sought to promulgate a set of values holding that each individual is simply "a cog in the big machine."

On its face, that idea seems to fit well with the Confucian concept of the submission of the individual—a concept the Chinese support less than the Japanese, who she says give it "a little too much" attention. In fact, however, the idea flies in the face of a simple capitalist fact: the Chinese, essentially entrepreneurial, "like to be small business owners."

A fourth aspect of Confucian teaching, and one of the most powerful, governs human relationships. Cheng notes that Confucius definitively laid down the correct relationship between ruler and ruled, ruler and minister, parents and children, husband and wife, and brother and sister. These teachings, she says, "still touch everybody's life."

Nowhere is this conflict of Confucianism and communism more evident than in the infamous one-child-per-family law. The regulation was imposed by the communists to stem a population crisis that adds more than 20 million babies each year to a nation already numbering 1.2 billion. But it comes squarely into conflict with the Confucian tenet that the man has a duty to produce a male heir to carry on the family name. Result: China officially has a far greater preponderance of baby boys than the statistical averages for the rest of the world.

Some baby girls, Cheng notes, are killed at birth so that the parents can try again for a boy. But a large number, she says, are kept in hiding. Evidence: by the time children reach school age, the numbers of boys and girls are found much more nearly equal. Peasants in rural areas, disliking the law, send pregnant wives to neighboring villages—where the local communist officials, having no interest in registering a newborn outsider, don't bother to ask whether the mother already has a first child. Cheng estimates that there are several million unregistered children in China today.

If the underlying values of Confucianism are still so strong, what will be their impact on China's future? Cheng, convinced that China is fundamentally and irreversibly changing, sees these values showing up in numerous ways.

"I am a pessimist in the short term, but not for the long term," says Cheng. She expects hard times to continue for as long as Deng Xiaoping and the current octogenarian leadership remain in place—a situation, she feels certain, that cannot last for many more years.

What happens after that? When a new group of leaders assumes power, she foresees that they will be weaker than their predecessors and will start by giving "concessions to the people." She notes that there is already "a pool of reformers in government" who are thoroughly conversant with conditions in the West and well aware of the collapse of Soviet communism. And while the Soviet communists and their Chinese counterparts parted ways and eventually became bitter antagonists, the Soviet collapse has made China's current leaders "very, very nervous."

What will be the effect on a new generation of leaders? "I think it is inevitable that socialism will be a thing of the past," she says. "I hope there will not be a bloody revolution, because China has had too many upheavals in modern times."

"If China could have ten years of a capitalist economic system, China could really take off," she says. While the result might not be a China reborn as a "first-class power," it would clearly, in her eyes, spell much greater prosperity for the people.

Is there widespread hope for such a change? Cheng points to evidence from several directions. The peasants, she says, continue to have more than one child—apparently counting on the fact that, before their newborns hit school age, they can become legitimate citizens.

She also notes that the residents of Hong Kong, the prosperous capitalist colony scheduled to revert to China from Britain in 1997, are not fleeing as fast as might be expected. Why not? "Because they are banking on China having a change," she says.

But couldn't that change return China to a neo-Maoist dictatorship with a reinvigorated communism? "No," she says simply. "The whole idea of communism has been discredited." Only by advocating "a whole new set of values, not communism," could a new dictator arise.

That does not mean that political repression won't recur. Noting that human rights abuses are still frequent in China, she observes that "what I went through can happen—and it is happening now." And she admits that a "strong man like Mao" can "make [the] whole nation mesmerized," leading people to believe that he really can improve the nation's status and prosperity.

She notes, however, that the desperate economic conditions that fostered communism are no longer present. "For the general public who are not in prison, life is much, much better," she says. "There is a plentiful food supply."

She also feels that the isolationism upon which Mao depended is a thing of the past. "China's economy cannot exist any more without trade with other nations," she says. Such trade is already occurring—not only with Western nations, where China's imbalance of exports over imports has created widely discussed difficulties, but also in less well known ways along the former Soviet border. There, she says, barter arrangements swell economic relations far beyond the official trade figures, as the Russians send raw materials and the Chinese return much-needed radios, calculators, garments, and food. Another export, however, may be even more important: Russian television programs, popular on the Chinese side of the border, are causing that once-closed nation to "enter into a totally new age" without even realizing it.

In the coming "new age," will China fly apart into separate smaller nations along the model of the former Soviet republics?

Cheng does not think so, although she sees some adjustments coming. "When the old people die and the weak successor comes along," she says, "I envision that inevitably Inner Mongolia will want to be united with Outer Mongolia—which is already adopting a market economy."

She also sees Tibet, an essentially religious country ravaged during the Cultural Revolution, breaking away. In addition, the ethnic groups in northwest China, who are largely of Russian extraction, will probably unite with their "compatriots across the border" and some regions near Vietnam may join that nation.

But the bulk of the Chinese territory, in her view, will remain a single nation—bound together by its residual Confucianism, its common Mandarin language (which she credits the communists with popularizing), and the racial homogeneity arising from the fact that most of China is inhabited almost exclusively by the Han Chinese.

Whichever way China goes, Cheng sees its direction being guided by its underlying values system. That values system, Cheng ackowledges, played a crucial part in her own ability to survive more than six years of captivity during the Cultural Revolution. Her survival, as she regularly tells student audiences on her lecture tours, owes a great deal to moral clarity.

"It was very important for me to know what was right and what was wrong—and not compromise with what is wrong," she recalls. Had she provided the "confession" her captors wanted—which would have made it easier for them to accuse Shell Oil, and by extension the entire Western commercial enterprise, of conspiring against China—she would have received better treatment and probably even have been released.

Instead, she was denied food and medicine, kept in cold, dark cells, beaten and tortured, and held in such utter isolation that "for six and one-half years I did not see a smiling face or hear a friendly voice." She knew, however, that she could "never compromise," because she would not be able to "face herself" if she did.

If her Confucian upbringing helped instill a sense of self-responsibility, Cheng gives even stronger credit to her Christian faith. Though she describes the Chinese as "not very religious"—held together "spiritually" by "a set of moral codes rather than by religion"—Cheng herself converted to Christianity after her marriage.

"My religious belief helped me a great deal" in prison, she says. There, she prayed regularly at night—going back over the events of each day and asking for guidance.

"I did not ask for a miracle," she recalls. "I asked that I be given intellect and courage—sufficient intellect so that

I can cope with this very complicated situation, and also the courage so that I do not fear death."

"I wasn't afraid to die if they should decide to kill me. Nevertheless, I did everything possible to keep alive—so that in the end I would clear my name.

"I believe that the burden rests with me—it was my responsibility to clear my name. They didn't succeed in confusing me: I knew that they were wrong."

Are there lessons from her experience relevant to the challenges facing today's society?

"I think people tend to be confused because we are bombarded with different views all the time," she says. Although she is now a U. S. citizen, Cheng is no blanket apologist for Western culture. She worries that the West—and the United States in particular—is far too "ready to abdicate" the high ground of values and ethics.

Needed, she says, is a much greater willingness on the part of parents to provide guidance to children—who, without it, are "bewildered."

"We could get rid of a lot of this drug problem if the parents would only instill in the mind of the child the concept of what is right and what is wrong from a very early age," she says. "The best way to do that is to set an example. I think that a lot of our social problems are due to the fact that the parents have abdicated their position."

Such guidance, however, will not work if it is stern and unloving. "You cannot guide without love," she says, "In fact, to guide your child is a sign of love."

What, finally, would she say to the next generation about

the core values necessary for survival? Her answer summarizes her experience as a survivor.

"One should basically know what is right and what is wrong—and, when you know that, be courageous enough to stand for what is right," she says. "That is the way to live—not to compromise with what is wrong."

executive director from 1980 to 1988, after five years as director of information and public affairs for the UN's Population Fund.

Born in what was then the British Commonwealth dominion known as Ceylon, Vittachi was raised as a Southern Buddhist—an important distinction, he notes, since, unlike its northern counterpart, Southern Buddhism "does not speak of God." At sixteen, as a university student at the University of Ceylon in Colombo, he became a communist. In 1953, at age thirty-five, he had become senior editor of Asia's oldest newspaper, the *Ceylon Observer*—a position, he says, that "wielded a lot of power." It was then, he recalls, that he began asking himself what all this power was for—feeling that "unless one knew what life was for, so that you could use your power well, you were just feeding your own ego."

Shortly afterward, he recalls, he had an experience he describes as "almost like an inward revelation" that caused him to seek "the meaning of the power that people called God." Joining with others in a movement of spiritual brotherhood called Subud, he recognized that his experience had begun to "change my entire thought patterns," until he found communism "unendurable" and broke from it. Later, his spirited defense of his nation's minorities caused him to be banished from Sri Lanka.

Vittachi has been a special correspondent for the *Economist*, the *Sunday Times* (London), and the BBC, and was a cofounder of the Press Foundation of Asia. Winner of the prestigious Ramon Magsaysay Award for Journalism in

1959, he is currently a columnist for *Newsweek International.*

An active member in the Global Forum of Spiritual and Parliamentary Leaders, he now reads the New Testament—"at least one chapter, usually John," he says—each week. He is the author of several books, including *The Brown Sahib* and *The Brown Sahib Revisited,* as well as *A Memoir of Bapak,* the founder of the Subud movement. After many years in New York, he now lives with his wife in Bangkok.

●　●　●

Asked to describe the elements of a global code of ethics, Tarzie Vittachi lifts the question to an entirely new plane. For him, the point is not only ethics, but man's search for meaning.

"I think that any code of conduct must be based on an understanding of the need for relationships," he says. "Nothing has any meaning unless it is a relationship: I cannot see myself as a person, feel myself as a person, unless I have a relationship with myself. And unless individuals find an identity, they cannot relate to other people."

Why is this point so important? Because, he says, "human relationships have got so fouled up" by individuals who have ignored their importance. "This applies not only to individuals," he explains, "but to a collection of individuals in a nation. Unless a group of people who comprise a nation can find their own identity and are comfortable with that identity, they cannot relate to other people—and this is the basis of war."

This failure of meaningful relationship, he feels, is at the heart of the major challenges facing humanity today. "We cannot find any meaning in all this talk about environmental pollution and increasing degradation unless we learn to relate to our ambiance. We cannot even find a meaningful life—the whole festoon of events that lead from infancy to death, the meaning of the passage of time—unless we predict within some sort of cosmic context that people have another life beyond this life and so look for that kind of relationship. For me, religion means a system of relationships. That is why every tradition has a behavioral code."

The Buddhist code under which he was raised, he recalls, was short and simple. It consisted of five *seelas*, or laws, repeated daily and meant to enforce the basic social relationships. The first element of "our daily prayer," he says, is, " 'I shall not kill.' "

"The second is, 'I shall not steal,' because stealing demeans me. Then, 'I shall not be sexually promiscuous'—that is, not frowning on sex, but on promiscuity, since that again demeans the people who engage in it. 'I shall not lie' has the implication of not telling unnecessary lies, [although] small lies, white lies prevent one from hurting one another. And then, 'I shall not drink to the point of excess'—not a ban on drinking, but on intoxication."

The underlying message of Buddha's code, says Vittachi, is moderation. "If we could practice some of these, if not all of these, every day, I think our lives would be very, very different."

Vittachi acknowledges that "every other religion" has something very similar. But such teachings, he feels, have declined in authority because of "the increasing secularization of the world, the increased mechanization of the world since the time of Galileo and certainly after Newton." With the advent of the conception of man as "just a combination of atomic particles, devoid of this unseen, untouchable thing called soul," people moved "away from religion to reason—depending entirely on a rational capacity to find out how to behave."

The result: *value* was replaced by *price* as the determinant of worth—a point, he says, cleverly made by the nineteenth-century British playwright Oscar Wilde, who defined a cynic as "a man who knows the price of everything, and the value of nothing." In that cynicism, he notes, religion became "pragmatic." It's a word he finds interesting because, in its original meaning, it meant *skilled in the affairs of state*—since the state, he explains, "has no morals" but only "interests."

"One man in the twentieth century, however, led us back into morality as a practical thing and not as a cloud-cuckoo-land idea, and that was Mohandas Gandhi." His greatest contribution to the discussion of politics and morality, says Vittachi, was his insistence that "the distinction that the Cartesians and the Marxists had made between *ends* and *means* was a false distinction." Gandhi demonstrated that "the means *were* the end—that how you did things determined the end, that violence as a means to solving a problem was in fact the nature of the solution. He was able to destroy the mightiest empire in history without the use of a single

221

gun. So the proof he gave was that morality was not impractical, and that what is practical and worth practicing is *only* morality."

It was, in fact, this ends-versus-means argument that drove Vittachi out of communism at the age of thirty-five. At one point, he recalls, "my communist teacher, my cell leader, asked me to steal a book we needed—to pick up a copy of one of Trotsky's books from a fellow teacher and friend who refused to lend his books. I was asked to steal it—for a 'good' end. That kind of thing made me sick."

He still retains, however, a conviction that the collective interests of society must take precedence over those of the individual. To create a meaningful future, he says, humanity will need to move from "unbridled competition" to cooperation, from nationalism to nonnationalism, and from the individual to the collective. It will require, he admits, "an enormous leap." But "that is what is demanded of us now: putting our community first, meaning the earth first, and all living things."

Vittachi's prescription for such change involves some form of world government. "One of the things that has to change is the notion that the nation-state is an efficient unit of human management. It stopped being efficient a long time ago. Yet we make children assume that nationality, nationalism, patriotism are the highest values."

Needed, instead, is "a supernational government" that involves "pooling sovereignty, surrendering a part of one's sovereignty." That doesn't mean, he hastens to add, "a homogenized world," but will require "preserving the wonderful variegation of cultures."

Does the United Nations supply the model for such world government? Vittachi, who is a strong believer in the U.N. activities, does not think so. "The United Nations is a pyramid of cowardice," he laments, which has been corrupted by "our self-serving ideas." It was founded, he points out, on the basis of individual nations trying to protect themselves—"not pooling of sovereignties," but "competitive sovereignties."

A better model, he feels, may be found in the European Common Market, in the Association of South East Asian Nations (ASEAN), and in other confederations that may emerge among formerly sovereign nation-states. Even India, whose "gigantism" has proved problematic for its Asian neighbors, may be breaking up into a "loose confederation." The result, he hopes, will be "a new kind of inter-regionalism that will evolve toward a global planet."

"I think we have the minds and the means to conceive such an idea—to make the necessary institutional frame that can operate," he says. But to do so, "the first value has to be that we are beings of one planet, and it is up to us as a responsible collective to look after one another, to look after minority interests, [which is always] the first duty of the majority."

What happens if, instead, we go into the twenty-first century with the values of the twentieth century?

"I feel it will be disastrous," he says. "The last century has actually been a very cruel century—no century has ever killed so many people at war, most [of them] civilians. I think all of us hope that the next century will be better for our children. But it can't be on the basis of there being a billion [people] destitute on the planet right now. Not just poor people—there are *three* billion poor people—but *destitute*, complete hopelessness. That is not a firm platform on which to launch a new century."

The next ten years, he says, should be spent "in search of the moral underpinnings that give better meaning to the new century." That involves much more than "just the negative business of trying to save the planet from self-destruction," but the positive and proactive desire to "make a better planet for human beings to live in responsibly."

Perhaps the most pressing issue along that line, says Vittachi, concerns population growth. "It is not just a question of reducing fertility," he says, but of understanding that even if all the family-planning programs in the world were 100 percent successful, "there will be a billion new customers, people coming into this world" in the early years of the twenty-first century.

"It's rather like you receiving a telephone call saying that your relatives in Arizona have lost their house in an earthquake and are on their way [to live with you]. Are you going to say, 'No'? Or are you going to rearrange your lives so that you can accommodate them. That is how we should be spending our time—not moaning about high population growth. The population problem will never be solved in the uterus, but in the human mind."

But can such changes be made?

With a smile, Vittachi recalls Dr. Samuel Johnson's well-known remark that "when a man knows he is to be hanged in a fortnight, it concentrates his mind wonderfully." Today, he says, "that is what has happened. People have suddenly become aware of the extraordinary chance of monumental self-destruction."

But even that may not be enough. "I think," concludes Vittachi, speaking from the perspective of his own profession of journalism, "that we generally have to be much more openly engaged in advocacy than we are willing to do now." The current concept of reporting—that it should be objective, factual, and aloof—simply will not be good enough, given the challenges of the future.

"We can't pretend that we are just holding up the mirror to reality and are not engaged—that we are just disinterested observers. All our lives, all our children's lives, are affected."

Astrid Lindgren

The Ethics of Pippi Longstocking

Love, yes. This is the main word for what we need—love on all stages and with all people.

W hen Astrid Lindgren describes how she came to write *Pippi Longstocking,* she links it to the overcoming of twin adversities.

The author of this Swedish children's classic recalls that the book began when her seven-year-old daughter, Karin, was sick with pneumonia and begged her mother to tell her stories. Asked what she wanted to hear, the child replied, "Tell about Pippi Långstrump"—Swedish for "long stocking," a name invented off the top of her head right at that moment.

So her mother began, and the tale grew through successive retellings over the next several years. Then came the second adversity: a fall on the ice outside her home in Stockholm in March 1944 that kept Mrs. Lindgren in bed for several weeks with a sprained ankle. To pass the time, she began writing down the tale of Pippi in the shorthand she used in her career as a stenographer. In May, for Karin's tenth birthday, she gave her daughter the manuscript. The next year, after some revision, it won first prize in a contest for children's books mounted by a Swedish publisher, Rabén and Sjögren, which published it with immediate critical acclaim and popular success.

Since then, Lindgren has written some fifty children's books and received numerous prizes, among them the Hans Christian Andersen Award and the Swedish Academy's Gold Medal. She has also played a central role in the development of children's literature, serving Rabén and Sjögren from 1946 to 1970 as their editor in charge of children's books. Among her favorite books: A. A. Milne's *Winnie the Pooh.*

A widow with seven grandchildren and six great-grandchildren, Lindgren lives in a cheery Stockholm apartment overlooking a park just up the street from a busy grade school. The interview, during which she spoke in deliberate but articulate English, was held in her book-lined living room hung with paintings with rural motifs.

• • •

To talk to Astrid Lindgren about the ethics of the future is to talk, quite naturally, about the next generation.

"For children I can always write," she says, noting that "a child is a child" today just as was the case in her own childhood. "As a child, I was very happy, and I remember everything about how it is to be a child."

"But I don't remember about my teenager years," she says, admitting that she could not write for today's teenagers. "I don't know them," she says simply, adding that "you must know what you write about."

She recalls that one of her first books after *Pippi Longstocking* was written for teenagers. Since that time, however, she feels teenagers have changed—not only in her native Sweden but across the world. "I think it's always very hard to be a teenager," she says sympathetically. But today in particular, she says, "they are a strange lot of people. They have other interests. They are more secure about themselves, and they think they can do what they want." And while that independence is not all bad, it often leads them to be "more critical of older people."

To some extent, says Lindgren, that criticism is deserved, given the lack of compassion and rigidities of attitude sometimes evident in the older generations. Yet Lindgren sees much in her own upbringing, and in the standards she was expected to obey, that calls forth her admiration. Again and again, in her writing and conversation, she returns to the discussion of the values that hold families together and help stabilize and inform the next generation.

"I think that if you could take the best of the ethics of

yesterday and mix it with the ethics of today when it is at its best, then it would be something very fine."

What were the "ethics of yesterday"? In her day, she recalls, "We were told what was right and what was wrong, and we were more—I wouldn't say that we were *better* than [teenagers] are now, but we had another situation."

Central to that "situation," she recalls, was the strong sense of family that came down to her not by teaching or preaching but simply by example. Crucial to that example, she feels, was the love and affection of her parents, Samuel August Ericsson and his wife, Hannah.

"I had a wonderful father," she recalls. A farmer who rented land from a local vicar, he was "a loving father— everybody loved him, and he had no enemies." Describing her parents in a memoir she wrote titled *Samuel August from Sevedstorp and Hannah of Hult,* she recounted that he fell in love with his wife-to-be when he was thirteen and she was nine. "He was very full of love for my mother," she says. Despite his background in a farming culture where affection typically gets little verbal expression, Lindgren remembers that he often told her mother how much he loved her. "We children were used to seeing our father holding his arms around our mother at least once a day," she says with a girlish laugh.

He was not, she recalls, a strict disciplinarian. "But that was natural," she says, noting that the four children—there were three sisters and a brother—had plenty of freedom and could "play and play" in the large areas surrounding the farm in those years leading up to World War I. "But we also had to learn to work, because on the farm it was necessary that everybody learned to work."

Only three times in her childhood, she recalls, did she ever get punished, "and that was by my mother." One time, she and her sister walked a considerable distance to their aunt's house, having been told by their mother to be home by seven o'clock. "But we had croissants, and we had a wonderful time. And I said to my aunt that I was so tired, and she said, 'You had better stay here overnight.' "

Having no telephone, it was impossible to ring their mother about the change in plans—and at ten o'clock, one of the farm hands sent by the worried parents came with a horse and wagon. "When we got home, mother said, 'Is it seven o'clock now?' And then we got spanked with a switch—it was a lousy one, because it broke when she tried to smash my legs. Otherwise we never had corporal punishment."

That sense of an affectionate and unpunishing family, and of a freedom for highly imaginative play, clearly set the pattern for Pippi—a red-headed, freckled nine-year-old with one stocking much longer than the other. Pippi's mother died when she was a baby and is now, she feels sure, "an angel in heaven." Her sea-captain father was washed overboard in a storm and, in Pippi's mind, is now "king of a cannibal island." She lives alone in her father's house in a rural village, with a trunk full of gold pieces he left behind that assures her independence and undergirds a life given over to zany, iconoclastic fun. She is also, as it happens, stronger than anyone in the world—"she could lift a whole horse if she wanted to." But in her many escapades—out-

231

witting policemen sent to put her in an orphanage, confront-ing a bull charging one of her friends, breaking up a band of bullies tormenting a smaller child, saving children from a burning building—she never uses her strength for any-thing but good.

And that, according to Lindgren, is significant. Pippi "never misuses her power," says the author. Although "she lives alone and she can do whatever she wants" undisciplined by the adult world, she never harms others. That fact is one of the "very important" ideas in Lindgren's code of ethics for the next century—"that you can have power, but you need not misuse it."

Another central idea, Lindgren observes, is obedience, a theme that runs through *Pippi Longstocking* from start to finish, though often upside down. "I think the teenagers of my years were very much more obedient," says Lindgren. Reflecting on that early training, she doesn't feel it was "nec-essarily very good to be so obedient"—a sentiment with which Pippi herself would have no trouble agreeing—and notes that "maybe it's better now in some ways." But she is concerned that in many cases today's young people "do what they want" without much adherence to standards. She also notes that they have much more money to spend than her generation ever had, and that some of them spend it on alcohol and drugs.

Adding to her list, Lindgren turns to questions of caring and unselfishness—"to take care of other people, and to take care of nature—to take care of a lot of things," she says. She recalls reading something from Marcus Aurelius, which she translates as, " 'Don't live as if you had a thousand

232

years ahead of you. Death is soaring over your head, so as long as you live, as long as you really can, be good.' "

"That is very plain," she says. "If you can live up to that, I think you know what is right and what is wrong."

Another candidate for her list is truth telling, which she defines as "to be honest, not lying, not afraid to say your opinion." Reminded that Pippi regularly told wild fabrications, Lindgren notes that "she is not lying in the way that I mean. She's honest, but she is telling stories," just as authors create fiction "without being liars." The distinction, for Lindgren, lies in the purpose. Pippi's tall tales are abundant and wacky, ranging from simple assertions like "in Egypt everybody walks [backward]" to the extended and richly allegorical tale of Malin, the grandmother's maid, who among other things systematically used Tuesday to break china, which the grandmother then replenished every Wednesday. Pippi, says Lindgren, tells tales "to amuse herself, and to amuse other people," but with no intent to deceive or defraud. "I think she had a good character," says her creator.

Lindgren is also concerned about the upsurge of violence, especially as it affects children. She sees the problem arising in several ways: among adults who abuse children in ways "so terrible that you can't hear it without crying," and among youngsters who, even in comparatively peaceful Sweden, sometimes kill one another with knives.

What should the adult world say in the face of such violence?

"I don't think it's any use to *say* things, but to *live* with children. If they see their parents living in peace with one another, and not punishing children bodily—if they have a happy childhood with no abuse from the parents, I think it is very hard to think that they would go and hurt someone with a knife."

"There comes a lot of cruelty into the world when [people] are very poor and have no work," she says. "They get disturbed, the adults, and they often take it out on the children. But the answer is love."

It is love, in fact, that knits together the various elements of her code of ethics. "Love, yes," she says. "This is the main word for what we need—love on all stages and with all people. Anybody who hasn't ever got any love can't be something else but"—she pauses to find the fitting English word—"a hooligan."

"I will tell you what I think about ethics," she concludes. "I think, 'To your own self be true.' Even for teenagers."

And what does "self" mean? "That you know who you are," she replies, "and you don't try to be somebody else."

Which sounds, not surprisingly, like Pippi herself talking.

Sergio Muñoz

The Universe of Morality

*Total freedom cannot exist when there is not
total equality.*

Ask Sergio Muñoz whether he has enjoyed his position as executive editor of *La Opinion*, the largest
Spanish-language daily newspaper in the United
States, and his animated features break into an infectious
grin.

"I am the happiest person on earth!" exclaims Muñoz,
a Mexican national who moved to Los Angeles in the 1970s
to pursue a Ph.D. in philosophy at the University of South-

ern California in Los Angeles. "I love every single minute of it."

Why? Because "the first duty of a journalist is to tell the truth. You have to give everyone a chance to give his point of view, and you should be as objective as you can be." That sort of journalism, he explains, is possible in the United States but was difficult to pursue in Mexico, where Muñoz began working in newspaper management after studying at the National University of Mexico and in London and Paris.

"I disliked the Mexican press profoundly," he recalls, "because it is a press that is always subject to the government."

The son of an industrialist father and a mother who was a teacher, Muñoz studied at the National Autonomous University of Mexico and the London School of Film Technique in the 1960s. He began his writing career as a copy writer for an advertising agency in Mexico City, rising quickly to the position of creative director. He lives with his wife and their two teenage children in Orange County, keeping in close touch with Mexico through frequent visits.

This interview took place in 1990 in his office at *La Opinion*. He has since served as executive news director for KMEX-TV in Los Angeles, the leading Spanish-language station in the United States.

●   ●   ●

When the letter came asking Sergio Muñoz to participate in an interview on ethics, the scholar-editor did two things: he went to his bookshelf to consult works on philosophy he hadn't opened in a decade, and then he called some of his best friends "to share with them my thoughts."

Those thoughts, expressed during a two-hour conversation in his downtown Los Angeles office next to the babble of the newsroom, underlie his conviction that, throughout history and across cultures, "moral values have remained the same."

"It really doesn't matter whether you are Muslim or Christian or Jew," he says. "In every religion, in every country, in every region at every time, there are some basic principles." Deep down, he says, "we all know what *good* is, what *correct* is, what *obligatory* is—all those things that compose ethics. They are the same."

Basic to that common code, he feels, are three elements best articulated in the motto of the French Revolution: *liberté, égalité, fraternité.*

• *Equality.* Of first importance, for Muñoz, is the concept of equal treatment. Morality, he notes, "is a social affair: it doesn't do any good for me to *be* good if I don't *do* good actions to someone. So the universe of morality is society."

Most immigrants, he feels, are drawn to the United States by the promise of equality. Whether they hope to be better off economically or politically, they are coming for equality of opportunity. "You don't want to be *put* somewhere," he says, speaking for the immigrant. "You don't want to be *placed*. You want to have the same opportunity as everyone."

Unfortunately, however, the "history of the Chicano people" has not always been one of encountering such opportunities in the United States. The reason: arriving as immigrants, they find "two Americas." One, he explains, is "very open and generous and warm, and wants to understand the plight of [other] people." The other, by contrast, is "closed" and "wants to keep things as they are."

That's not a uniquely American phenomenon, he admits, noting that Mexico is much the same way. But the problem for the Latin American immigrant to the United States is compounded by the vast differences in development between the two. "Many times the trip is not only from south to north, but it is also from the nineteenth century to the twenty-first," he notes.

But such differences tend to obscure a fundamental point, which is that "the people who come from Mexico and El Salvador have the same values, in my point of view, as the person that comes from Minnesota or from Alabama or from California—those basic principles that are common to all civilizations. And I deliberately don't say 'Western civilization,' because I think they are common to all civilizations."

Despite this commonality, however, these values may take different forms, depending on "a mixture of your own upbringing, your own culture, with the culture you are facing." And while the result may seem to be markedly different sets of values held by different groups, they spring from commonly held beliefs, within which, he concludes, "the pursuit of equality is basic."

• *Fraternity.* The French word for *brotherhood*, says Muñoz, is called *solidarity* in Mexico, as it is in Poland. But what exactly does it mean? That question, he says, is "something I face quite often" as a Mexican living in the United States.

"For the Americans, I am Mexican," he says with a chuckle. "But for Mexicans, I am the one that got away. Sometimes I am a traitor, sometimes I am a human being. It depends on the emotions of the person who is judging."

"There are a lot of things that are common between Mexico and the United States. And there are many opportunities to bridge gaps. Look at what happens between Tijuana and San Diego. Look what happens between [other] border towns. They are interlinked.

"So my wish for my code of ethics is that there be cooperation, instead of believing that the only way that I can prosper is by defeating you, by competing with you, by antagonizing you. The way we are both going to succeed is by joining forces even if we are different, even if you are blonde and I am dark. Let's look for those deep things in common."

• *Freedom.* Central to the expression of both equality and fraternity is the *liberté* or freedom that makes them possible. Without the freedom to practice equality and fraternity, he says, ethics "becomes just theory, rhetoric."

Freedom, however, has multiple meanings. "Sometimes I feel exasperated by the abuse of the word 'freedom' here in the United States. Americans look at themselves as the freest of the free—and sometimes it gets nauseating, because it is not the truth. I think that total freedom cannot exist when there is not total equality."

"If you could listen to the horror stories that I have to

listen to—people who are making the trip, or people who are born here but are dark-skinned—they are treated like second-class citizens."

For many, then, freedom is little more than a "high-rhetoric statement." And while that statement serves a useful purpose—in "making people believe that they are free, so they become freer than so many people that I know in Mexico"—the fact remains that in order to be genuinely free "we have to be equal."

These core values of equality, fraternity, and freedom are nevertheless subject to varying applications. "The basic values are the same," he reiterates. "What changes are the fashions." Case in point: the history of the United States.

In the early days of the nation, he says, "people were pitching in together, making this paradise on earth—as long as you were white." The idea was that "to build this country, there will be some sacrifices, but in the end we're all going to survive." The result was what he calls the "very strict rules" of the Protestant work ethic, which he paraphrases as "you have to work and work and work and work and work—and eventually when you retire you will be able to climb the pyramids of Egypt."

But in the 1960s, he says, "people started looking inwards and saying, 'Now I must have some self-fulfillment, I must have fun. I mean, why work so hard? I gotta climb the pyramids *now* while I'm young.' So there was a change in the world, and here in the States it's a big, big, big, *big* change."

In those years, he says, society clearly became "more hedonistic." But the change was more of fashion than of

fundamental moral principles. "Whether you believe in sac-
rifice or in seeking pleasure," he explains, "you always know
that it is wrong to kill someone. You always know that it is
incorrect to abuse someone, to take advantage of something.
I think the basic principles of civilized life remain the same.
And the inner self that tells you *I shouldn't do this!* is the
same whether you are a hedonist or a sacrificer."

Then has society become less ethical over time?

"No, not at all. Let me give you an example—it may
sound a little bit anti-American, but it's not. In the old days,
if Teddy Roosevelt said, 'Let's go and invade Colombia and
create Panama,' the United States would say, 'Yeah, let's go
and do it!' Now if the United States goes to Vietnam or
invades Panama or Grenada, there's going to be a part of
America that's going to say, 'No! That's not right! We have
no business being there!'

"A society where self-criticism is exercised so much, as
here in the States, has not changed its ethical values. They
are the same. And maybe now we are listening to more
voices because it's a multiverse society, a more open
society."

Muñoz, however, remains deeply concerned about the
nation's ills. "I do not understand why America has this
voracious appetite for drugs, which I think are morally
wrong. And I still don't see why America must see itself as
the policeman of the world and try to tell everyone else how
to live. I think there are some signs of moral—I don't want
to say *decadence* because I don't think we're decadent—but
signs where morally [the country] is in a weak position. But
that does not mean at all that values have descended, have

decayed. It means the different forces of society fight. And sometimes these forces win and sometimes these other forces [win]."

What's the significance of all this for the twenty-first century? With a laugh, Muñoz notes that there's good news and bad news. The bad news has to do with immigration. "I think this is the only country in the world that boasts about being a country of immigrants. This is the only country in the world that smacks you in the face saying, 'Look! We got all the poor people of the world, and we began from scratch, and we are the newest country in the world.' "

"Now, these forces that created the country are still happening. There is still immigration from the European countries and the Asian countries and from Latin America. And there's a closed America that says, 'That's enough.' There are some people who believe that the cup runneth over, and that's it. I believe that's a big mistake."

On the other side, however, are those who understand that the real question for the twenty-first century can be simply stated: where is the work force of the future going to come from? With the average American family having one-and-one-quarter children, he says, "who is going to work so that they can get their Social Security checks in the year 2010? You know where it's going to come from? The immigrants. I don't think the country is running out of space. I don't think the country is running out of resources. And I think the immigrants may save it."

For Muñoz, then, the choice is not whether there will be immigrants but how the nation deals with them—whether through regulating the influx and letting them "live in ghettos" with "a little bathroom" until the pressures grow intolerable and some form of rebellion breaks out, or through educating them to be valuable contributors to the nation.

"The second scenario is the one in which America triumphs," he says. "It says, 'Look, we need these guys. Let's teach them how to do things, so that they can progress. The more *they* progress, the more *we* progress.' Here again we come to fraternity. And again we come to equality of opportunities."

In this version of the future, says Muñoz, there is no need for fenced and gated communities patrolled by dogs sitting side by side with "the belt of poverty that surrounds the barrio." That, he says, is the vision of "the kind of America that I love and that I am willing to work for and that I am committed morally to make happen."

How can this vision be taught? Through three institutions—church, school, and family—that Muñoz worries are "deteriorating within the Anglo-Saxon community" but remain strong among Hispanics.

"I don't think the church has lost its grip on the Hispanics. What we are facing is a fight between the Catholic and the Protestant church to see who gains the heart of the Hispanic community. Most of the people I know are very religious, either Catholic or Protestant."

The second institution, the school, remains for Hispanics "the most important nucleus" of the community. He notes that as a *social* institution, the schools are doing fine—already having a more than 60 percent Hispanic enrollment in Los Angeles. "What is wrong is the school as an *educational* institution. What we have to do is reform the educational system to force it to teach better."

And the family? Here Muñoz breaks into anecdote, recalling the many times he has driven by a "magnificent, gorgeous public park" in wealthy Orange County. The problem, he says, is that it is always empty—"all that water wasted keeping those lawns so green, and nobody uses them."

By contrast, he says, the parks in the barrios of East Los Angeles are full of families—grandparents, parents, children, and their relatives—having picnics. Driving past those parks, he says, assures him that "the family is not an institution that is dying with the Hispanics. It is alive and well and keeps us in touch."

It is that kind of community, he says, that produces the ethical individuals so needed by the world. What are the qualities of such people? After some reflection, Muñoz ticks off the attributes of the ethical person.

"Well, I would say that he is good. What I mean is that he is trying to do the best that he can for the most people. His attitude is not egotistical. He thinks, 'If I do this, then this many people will benefit.'

"He is not arrogant. He doesn't think he is something special. He thinks he is just another one that can do something good. He thinks that he is equal [to others]. He has knowledge and spreads it around. He would never harm anyone. And you feel comfortable being with him, whether you are a very poor peasant that just came from Mexico or El Salvador or whether you are a CEO of a big oil company. You feel warmth, and he makes you feel well."

So such a man fits the definition of ethics as liberty, equality, and fraternity?

"Yes—that's amazing!" says Muñoz, looking back over what he has just said and noting that he was "truly not trying to make a tie-in" with his earlier ideas. The point, he concludes, is simply that such an individual "is good because he does the most good to the most people."

Katharine Whitehorn

Morality for Nomads

*We are going to have to find an ethic which
says, 'Forget about whether you're on my side
or on their side: there are certain things that
people like me do not do.'*

If George Bernard Shaw had met Katharine Whitehorn,
he would have liked her immediately. Bright but consid-
erate, witty without cynicism, amiably balancing the pleasures of home and family with the demands of her position
as a widely respected senior columnist for the London
Sunday newspaper the *Observer*, she would have struck Shaw
as "liberated." Her liberation began early. Born in London,
she was educated at various schools, including Glasgow

High School for Girls and Roedean, from which she ran away. Before beginning her career in journalism, she taught English in Finland and worked as a graduate assistant at Cornell University.

Since then, her career has carried her to levels unimagined in Shaw's England. The first woman to become rector of St. Andrews University, she currently serves as vice president of the Patients Association and the Open Section of the Royal Society of Medicine. Author of several books aimed at giving information in a painless way, including *How to Survive Children* and *How to Survive Your Money Problems,* she was a member of the press corps on former Prime Minister Margaret Thatcher's first visit to China. In 1992, the International Women's Forum in Denver gave her its "Woman Who Makes a Difference" award. The mother of two grown sons, she now puts considerable energy into issues of marriage and family, serving as president of the Middlesex Marriage Guidance Counselors' Association.

Her home in the Chalk Farm section of London reflects her interests and character. On the desk in her study, occupying one end of her book-lined living room, is the aging portable typewriter on which she still pecks out her much-respected weekly columns. "My generation of women had to be lousy typists," she explains, noting that "it was the only way we got to do anything else." Now, seated before a fire, she seems perfectly comfortable with the fact that her husband, best-selling mystery writer Gavin Lyall, is busying himself in the kitchen below making dinner, despite the fact that she, not he, is the author of several widely used cookbooks.

Does she think of herself, then, as a feminist? Her reply recalls the novelist Rebecca West's comment that "while she wasn't sure what a feminist was, she was sure she always got called one whenever she said anything that distinguished her from either a doormat or a prostitute."

"I've become slightly more feminist as I get older," she says with a smile, "but I shy away from this label."

• • •

As she settles onto her sofa late on an October afternoon, Katharine Whitehorn recalls an incident that, for her, summarizes the shallowness of so much of today's thinking about morality and character.

An American, she says, was asked by an Australian why sports received so much attention in U. S. schools. Because, the American replied glibly, it is through sports that "you learn to work hard and do what you're told, and to put other people and the general interest ahead of what you might want to do yourself, and to set yourself a goal and get there."

"Yes," replied the Australian, "but these are exactly the qualities needed by a train driver to Dachau!"

The point, for Whitehorn, is that without a clearly moral purpose, even the best of today's education may contribute to developments as horrendous as that infamous Nazi concentration camp in World War II—and produce individuals incapable of resisting the ethical vacuums that produced it.

Scanning the moral landscape, Whitehorn sees few Dachaus looming on the horizon. But she worries that in three specific areas—environmental degradation, the growth of nationalism, and the challenges facing the family—humanity will need to define its ethics much more clearly for the twenty-first century.

• *Environmental degradation.* "I think the global ethical issues [for the next century] are going to concern themselves very strongly with the things that relate to the survival of the planet," she says. Some of these "green issues" are well known, including "the question of ivory, the question of the rain forest, the question of inappropriate technology."

Others, however, are less obvious. Europeans headed for Africa, for example, keep trying to take their cattle, which, in their struggle to survive, do serious damage to the African ecosystem. What's needed, she says, is to "try and work out why it is that [such native species as] the eland and the oryx survive the arid conditions where the European cattle can't." The answer, she says, has to do with such things as being able to feed at night when there is more water in the plants and "having better kidneys so they can get rid of waste products with very much less water loss." European cattle, by contrast, tend to dig deeper, diminish the water table, and add to the trend toward desertification.

The problem, in her view, is not the cattle but the Europeans. So how, she wonders, can people be made to think deeply and care fervently about the environment?

"I don't think that people habitually do anything," she says, "unless they are programmed so that they are appalled with themselves if they don't." Needed, she says, is some version of a "green religion" that elevates environmental issues to the level of "a Jew not eating pork."

By way of example, she describes her own efforts at recycling glass. "I take things to the bottle bank," she says, "but not if I'm in a hurry. If I thought I'd actually go to hell if I didn't take the bottles back, it might be different. I think that some form of ethic where, if you pollute the environment, [you earn] a kind of moral reprimand from your mates that you really pay attention to—I think that's going to be extremely important."

"Religions tend to have things that say, 'I will not do this because I am this sort of person.' Any religion, including ones I disapprove of, all have prohibitions."

She doesn't imagine, however, that elevating environmental issues to a quasi-religious level will be easy. Noting an issue currently in the news—the apparent murder-suicide of the leader of the German Green Party, Petra Kelly, and her longtime companion—Whitehorn points to press accounts attributing the deaths to Kelly's despair over public insensitivity to environmental concerns.

Reading such accounts, she says, "you might think it's all hopeless. I don't think so. If you look at the early Christians, they had a pretty thin time, too." She is encouraged to think that moral turnarounds can indeed occur: look, she says, at "the way it has become totally unacceptable in America to smoke."

Such a moral change will require not only a shift in behavior but in aspiration, reinforced by steady social pressure and discussion. And while the point is not to return to Victorian values—"Victorian England was an absolute sink!" she says—there is a need for the kind of aspiration toward goodness that was part of the Victorian rhetoric. "Whatever the Victorians did or didn't do," she says, "they were told each Sunday that this is something they were *supposed* to do."

• *The growth of nationalism.* Looking across the map of the world, Whitehorn is also concerned about the rampant increase in ethnic, tribal, and nationalistic conflict. Of the former Soviet satellites and republics, she notes, "there isn't a single country that doesn't have a very sizable minority of some other group—religious, or ethnic, or linguistic, or all three."

"Look what's happening in Eastern Europe," she says, where in every country people are "killing each other, or trying to, or working out a way to."

"I think a great many people thought, in the twenties and thirties, that we were moving away from small nationalisms. The idealistic side of communism—which was immense, although postwar Americans find that hard to believe—meant that we were all brothers [and that] all this nationalism and tribal warfare was from the dark ages and [had to be] put behind us."

What has happened in recent years, she says, is that "everybody's been made sadly aware that those little tribal rivalries don't go away that easily. What we're learning is that the feeling that 'This is my group!' is not easily obliterated. And we can see how totally destructive it is."

She is not, however, advocating a rigid ideology to replace a pervasive nationalism. Ideological fervor, in her view, has caused a great deal of today's misery. In the past, she notes, nations behaved "extremely badly, but there was a general idea that there was such a thing as 'rules of war.' " And while at times those rules merely provided an excuse for "killing more of the lower classes and sparing more of the gentry," it sometimes meant that combatants were able to say, " 'You're a brave soldier and I'm a brave soldier: you will give me your sword and surrender with dignity.' "

With the twentieth century, however, came "the war to end all wars, and the ideological wars. Once you get the ideological wars, you say, 'To hell with rules, we must stamp out Nazis at all costs.' Of course, the logical outcome is that you end up behaving as bad as the Nazis did. So what were you fighting for?"

"We are going to have to find an ethic which says, 'Forget about whether you're on my side or on their side: there are certain things that people like me do not do.' "

One road toward such an ethic, Whitehorn says, may lie in something she has often discussed with her son Bernard. "He invented the phrase *morality for nomads*," she says. By that, he means a morality suited to an age of mobility that "transcends one's tribal grouping without imagining that it's going to obliterate them." To some extent, the major world religions achieve that balance: "You may be a Pakistani and I may be Saudi Arabian," she says, "but we're all Muslims together in the brotherhood of Islam."

And while such communities of religion may not always have worked well, "they all had a theory that they at least ought to be nice to each other." That, for Whitehorn, is a good start, although true morality must go farther. "I think

255

you have to work toward not, 'We treat our own people well' but, 'Our honor is internalized in us and we do not do these things no matter what.' "

• *Challenges facing the family.* Central to Whitehorn's sense of ethics for nations are the values expressed within a family context. The challenges facing today's families, in her view, are largely reflected in the increasing prevalence of family breakup.

"From where I sit," she says, "an awful lot of the breakup of the American family, about which we are constantly hearing, is not because women have gone off and wanted to get educated and have jobs. It's because you can't rely on the men to stick around."

While she's not opposed to divorce—since "in any one individual case [it] may make very good sense indeed"—she would not be upset if divorces were "extremely difficult" to get, or if there were an "easy" divorce for marriages with no children and a "much stiffer contract" otherwise.

Yet under the current regime of easy divorce, she notes, "three out of five marriages are breaking up. So you can't say to your daughters, 'Put up with whatever he gives you,' because in the long run it's no good: there's a three-in-five chance he's going to push off. If you have a society that's very tolerant of divorce, you're inevitably going to get turbulence among the women, because you cannot enforce them sticking home and being homebodies and being provided for if the breadwinner's going to push off."

"If you have a society with no divorce at all, you'll have

some desperately unhappy people. If you have a society where it's up to 30 or 40 or 50 percent, there's something really wrong. It's a matter of proportion: if it's between 10 and 20 percent, that's probably about right."

Even if they stay married, however, women in the industrial nations also face particular pressures from a corporate climate that "deliberately keeps the chaps on the move so they can't get too attached to anything but the company." As a result, "the women have to somehow make a culture for the family, because the bloke is always off selling biscuits in Japan."

Such circumstances, she notes, bear an odd resemblance to the family patterns in primitive societies, where "the men were not there to be counted on a large amount of the time." In those cases, "you're much more likely to have the moral stability, if there is any, coming down through the female line. The women can't wait for [men] to come back and decree morality every now and then."

What, then, does all this mean for the much-touted concern for "family values," as that phrase appeared in American social rhetoric?

"It makes me think of the happy family—that you and I like—not so much as the only God-given way to proceed but as a luxury that it takes a certain self-structure to have at all."

For Whitehorn, that "self-structure" is based on such moral qualities as trust. "The idea that you ought to be able to trust somebody is out of fashion," she notes. Where in this situation, she asks, "are you going to get the individual morals from, the feeling of trust?" The answer, she says, is that it must come "from yourself internally," rather than from a "compact" or negotiated agreement with others.

It is for that point—the lack of trust—that Whitehorn reserves some of her most pungent criticism. The problem, she says, is especially pronounced in the commercial world. "I think we are totally lacking in any sort of corporate morality," she asserts. "We used to think that we had some kind of morality in the Stock Exchange—at least you didn't cheat your mates—but the events of the last ten years showed we don't even have that."

Her concern, however, goes beyond behavior and into language. She worries that the world of international commerce, because it depends on what she calls "the language of money," reduces human concerns for other aspects of life. "It is a crippling and inadequate language," she says, because those who depend on it often "don't have any proper vertical taproots" into their communities, their homes, and their families, and no way of discussing these things.

That lack of roots, she feels, can have troubling effects on society. "If the fifties was living on the religious moral capital of the prewar era," she says, "we are now living on the moral capital of the fifties and sixties," in which there was "an enormous amount of goodwill and idealism." By contrast, "the language [we're] all supposed to talk right now is the language of finance. Whether the idealism will survive a great flood of chat about balance sheets, I don't know."

Does that leave her hopeful?

"Not very," she fires back. Then, more reflectively, she observes that, with maturity, "one begins to realize the thing everyone hates to realize, [which] is that order has a value in itself."

Back in the sixties, she says, people had such a wonderful time because they were getting away from the material restrictions of the war and from its austerity. They were also, she admits, "getting away from their parents."

"Some of it was actually morality, but some was nothing of the sort—just malice. It was great fun to say, 'I'm not going to pay any attention to all that.'

"It's fun to break away. It's hard to grow up and have to put it together again."

SIX

Government and Politics
Upright Individuals

*The effect of one upright individual is
incalculable.*

—Oscar Arias

Oscar Arias

The Nation as Moral Power

*In the twenty-first century, survival will be a
more complicated and precarious question
than ever before, and the ethics required of us
must be correspondingly sophisticated.*

T he enemy is poverty around the world—and unless
you realize that, we'll have a very insecure world."
Lounging casually in a red leather chair in his
study, the former president of Costa Rica speaks deliberately, choosing his words with sober care. Indeed, everything about Oscar Arias suggests a single-mindedness of
purpose: even the books and journals strewn on his coffee
table focus on the intertwined themes of poverty, violence,

and instability in the developing world. Again and again during a forty-five minute conversation at his home in the capital city of San Jose, the conversation returns to a single overriding theme: the ethics of peace.

When he won the Nobel Peace Prize in 1987, in fact, prize-watchers around the world nodded knowingly. Costa Rica had reportedly been on the prize committee's list for years. After all, it had abolished its army in 1948—the first nation in modern times to do so—and had subsequently prospered as the "Switzerland of the Americas" even as its neighbors in Nicaragua and El Salvador were destroying themselves through warfare. The committee seemed only to be waiting for an individual to step forward and embody the pacifist and strongly democratic values of this nation of three million people.

In the end, Dr. Arias was the man. No sooner had he assumed office in 1986 than he waded into the Central American conflict with a peace plan that, contrary to the then-current U. S. policy of arming friendly forces in the region, emphasized negotiations over warfare.

"It wasn't easy for me to choose peace instead of violence," he recalls, "because I was strongly criticized for daring to disagree with President Reagan concerning his solution to the conflicts—that is, not supporting a military solution in Nicaragua but promoting dialogue and negotiation in order to find a diplomatic solution."

"So I used to say that we [in Costa Rica] were not an economic power and not a military power, but that we were a moral power—in the sense that the decisions I took were taken according to values, ideals, and principles . . . rather than opinion polls."

Risky though his move was, history proved Arias right: the process he initiated, propelled by the Nobel committee's award, ultimately resulted in elections in Nicaragua and the end of the war between the Sandinistas and the Contras. Since then, prevented by the Costa Rican constitution from serving another term as president—a regulation he strongly favors—Arias has used his prize money to establish the Arias Foundation for Peace and Human Progress to pursue issues of regional and global peace.

In keeping with his studious nature, Arias agreed to this interview only if the questions were made available ahead of time. He then crafted carefully written answers to each one. The following is an edited version of his responses.

If you could help formulate a global code of ethics for the twenty-first century, what would be in it?

"I would offer three principles as a way of summarizing the kind of ethical thinking that the challenges of the twenty-first century require: responsibility, respect, and individual conscience.

"Before saying more about these three principles, however, I would like to discuss the status of ethical standards. I believe that there is a genuine and universal basis for ethical values, which can be identified without ignoring the values of particular cultures and which can bind us together as the genuinely global community we must become. Let me explain.

"Human beings are fundamentally equal and rational, each with intrinsic value and individual needs, but all needing to coordinate their actions to survive and prosper. If we think of ourselves as ambitious but vulnerable, we can see that we could only agree to an ethics which would bar universal violence, coercion, and oppression as incompatible with the basic need for cooperation. We would also rely on principles of obligations to respect others and to contribute to communal development in some way, as necessary for the development and flourishing of each individual.

"Such a view gives us a way to speak confidently of an ethics that can be common to all the inhabitants of this tiny globe, while respecting the manifold ways that different cultures may embody and practice their own ethical beliefs. We need to see and to acknowledge the idea of global ethics as a shared and voluntary but permanent bond, rather than as something to be imposed on others or which has been imposed on us. In doing so there are two traps to avoid. On the one hand, we must not be insensitive or parochial. On the other hand, we must not fear to condemn unjust or oppressive practices."

Of the ethical precepts mentioned above, why do you think each is particularly important?

"*Responsibility* is fundamental to our interactions with one another in our daily lives. Families, workplaces, friend-

266

ships, and political communities would all collapse were it not for the responsibility each person takes on, acknowledges, and sees through. But paradoxically, responsibility is not often mentioned in discussions of world politics or ethics: there, the talk is all of rights, demands, and desires.

"Human rights *are* an unquestionable and critical priority for political societies and an indispensable lever for genuine development. But the important thing is not just to assert rights, but to ensure that they be protected. Achieving this protection rests wholly on the principle of responsibility.

"On this basis, each person is an agent who acts on behalf of others, prior to demanding that others act for his or her benefit. Our biological world is a world of interdependence, in which no organism is an island: the survival of each creature is bound up with the survival of an ecosystem in a complex and delicate balance.

"In such a world, isolated assertions of rights or needs have no place. The real and urgent needs of injustice and inequality must be addressed, but not as demands made by the unfortunate and met by the lucky out of guilt or prudence. Rather, they must be addressed from a standpoint of inescapable mutual interdependence. This concept of responsibility must be incorporated into our self-images as well as into our ethical and political discussions.

"*Respect* for oneself and others is the essential precondition for any ethical action. No one can be expected to act ethically if he or she has been treated as subhuman, or inadequate, or dispensable, or interchangeable with anyone else. Ethics begins with an acknowledgment of the universal condition of equal and vulnerable rationality, and this acknowledgment must include awareness of one's self as the equal of others. Our practices of schooling, of religious tolerance, of integration of refugees—all must incorporate the basic principle of self-respect for individuals as a precondition for their respect for others.

"In the political realm, respect for others is a way of spelling out the assumption of equality and of equal rights. We cannot and should not always treat everyone alike. But we must always treat everyone with equal respect in weighing political choices. If the principle of respect were taken seriously, I believe that many of the bitter conflicts wracking individual regions and countries, dividing ethnic or religious groups, and shattering families and communities could be resolved peacefully. Living together does not require that we be the same, but rather that we work to understand and respect one another's differences.

"Without the principle of *individual conscience,* every attempt to institutionalize ethics must necessarily collapse. The implosion of the former Soviet Union and its empire has shown us unforgettably the power of individual conscience to endure a corrupt political regime. Similarly, in Latin America the courageous protests of individuals have everywhere been essential to the end of military rule and the restoration of democracy.

"As my friend Vaclav Havel, the president of Czechoslovakia, has emphasized, totalitarian rule must ultimately fail because it does violence to the irreducible life-force of the individual conscience. We in Latin America have also learned this lesson from our own difficult history: no regime that suppresses individual conscience is worthy of a free people, nor can it create a lasting peace.

"Democracy cannot survive as a matter of institutions alone. It relies ultimately on the conscience and care of each citizen to prevent it from deteriorating into mere pacification of the majority or a cynical policy of self-aggrandizement. So individuals and individual choices *do* matter: the effect of one upright individual is incalculable. World leaders may see their effect in headlines, but the ultimate course of the globe will be determined by the efforts of innumerable individuals acting on their consciences."

How hopeful are you that each of these precepts can really be adhered to in the future? What are the dangers if they are not adhered to?

"I am an optimist by nature and deep conviction: I believe in the goodness of the human soul and in the reality of our impulses towards the good. But I do foresee great dangers and challenges to the acknowledgment of our global ethical responsibilities.

"The siren calls of greed, envy, and sheer power lure us to put our faith in weapons, not ethics; in warfare, not plowshares; in divisions and distrust rather than in interdependence and individual responsibility. These dangers—the appeal to narrowly conceived nationalism, to racist and mistrustful policies of exclusion, to technological destruction of natural balance—all threaten to overwhelm our attentiveness to the ethical principles that are embodied in the lives we live with our nearest intimates and tempt us to succumb to a view of *realpolitik* to deal with those who seem to be strangers.

"I believe we can overcome these temptations. We can invest our energies in working for and with one another rather than against one another. But to do so will require that we resist easy solutions to immediate economic hardship. The people must lead their leaders. Individuals must make clear that they will not be swayed by irresponsible appeals to envy, hate, and fear. They must insist that their political leaders respect and promote the values that make a shared life possible."

How important is sound ethics for our future? Is ethics simply a pleasant luxury, or will it be essential to good government in the twenty-first century?

"As I have been stressing, ethics is an indispensable framework for our view of ourselves and of others. The idea that ethics is a luxury results from a narrowly reductionist view that treats human problems as neutral scientific facts from which values can be excluded. This was a tenet of the positivist program for science, which seemed to promise a brave new world for human beings—a world based on dispassionate scientific analysis giving the truth to technocrats, who could then use science to make people better.

"But the terrible history of the twentieth century has taught us that if we allow organization and science to be detachable from human values, they can be used to murder as easily as to protect. In fact, when we speak of human beings and their interactions, values are not something extra and optional: they are constitutive of our action in the world, of the ways we find others intelligible, and of the responses we make to them. Thinkers as different as Max Weber and Ludwig Wittgenstein have converged in their insistence that the perception of value is *not* optional. It imbues the ways we structure, interpret, and act in the world.

"So the real question is not whether we *should* be ethical: no human society could survive without codes of acceptable behavior, sanctions, socialization, and structures. Rather, the real and urgent question is whether we can evolve an ethics commensurate with our rapidly increasing cognitive and technological powers and with the communications capabilities which give us unparalleled knowledge of the lives of distant strangers and how we affect them.

"Ethics is never dispensable. It is an integral part of human survival. But in the twenty-first century, such survival will be a more complicated and precarious question than ever before, and the ethics required of us must be correspondingly sophisticated."

Do you see an age of war or an age of peace ahead?

"I see before us neither an age of war nor an age of peace, but an age of *choice*. The twenty-first century is in our hands. We confront enormous dangers: global injustice, environmental crises, destructive nationalisms, arms production and trading, continued inequality in the status of women, people of color, and others who face discrimination and persecution. On the other hand, the breakup of the former Soviet Union has been an historic moment which we are privileged to have seen, and which has opened unparalleled possibilities for world change.

"The freedoms, as well as the problems, facing the new countries of the Commonwealth of Independent States and of Eastern Europe are detailed daily in the world press. Less familiar, perhaps, are the effects on Latin America. The collapse of communism has loosened the stranglehold of ideology on the conflicts in Central and South America. Freed from the rigid pressures of the Cold War, our sister countries in the Americas can start to address domestic problems in domestic terms—without the enticements and entanglements of outside superpowers."

What would you say to the young people of the twenty-first century about the importance of a high standard of ethics and how their own fundamental values will shape the future?

"I would want to say to them, Do not lose faith. Do not accept hatred as necessary or natural. Do not be satisfied with the claims that injustice is inevitable or poverty merely regrettable. If each young person learns to trust in his or her own conscience, the world will hear a clarion call for change that has never been equaled."

272

Salim El Hoss

Enlarging the Role of the Smaller Powers

*I think international law, regardless of how it
is conceived, should be inherently ethical. It has
to be legitimate to be really legal.*

I n the Arab world, few countries are more complex than
Lebanon. Torn from within by Muslim-Christian strife,
attacked and occupied from outside by Israel, the tiny
Middle Eastern nation seems a virtual anthology of animos-
ity. Once a sought-after resort destination among Arabs, it
now appears in the news largely as a haven for terrorists and
their hostages.

Of all the world's nations, then, it might seem an unlikely place to find a deep commitment to ethics. Yet twice in the last sixteen years—from 1976 to 1980 and from 1987 to 1990—a man widely admired among Arabs and Westerners for his ethical behavior has been Lebanon's head of state. Salim El Hoss, a quiet, scholarly man with an avuncular warmth and an infectious laugh, is a far cry from the battle-hardened military commanders of some neighboring states. A vegetarian who has never yet smoked tobacco nor tasted alcohol, he deplores violence. A Muslim who cherishes "the values of Islam"—especially the "call for peace and love and consideration for your neighbor and responsibility for your actions" that he says parallel the core values of Christianity—he is a former professor of business and current member of the board of trustees of the American University of Beirut.

El Hoss earned his Ph.D. in economics and business from Indiana University in 1961 on a Rockefeller Foundation scholarship. He served as chairman of the board of the Banque Arabe et Internationale d'Investissement in Paris from 1982 to 1985, and was head of the Arab Experts Team, commissioned by the Arab League, in 1986 and 1987. He has written widely on economics and politics, including two books in English and six in Arabic.

A widower whose daughter traveled with him on a month-long sojourn in 1992 in the United States and Canada, he feels strongly that "the home is the center of ethics in any society." During that trip, he agreed to discuss global ethics and the state of world affairs at the university's modest headquarters-in-exile in a New York City office building.

•　•　•

Midway through a highly focused seventy-five-minute interview with Salim El Hoss, the conversation turns to the
human tragedy and political dismemberment of the former
Yugoslavia—a situation news commentators sometimes describe as the "Lebanonization" of that Balkan nation.

El Hoss bursts into laughter at the word. "At one time,"
he recalls with ironic relish, "we [in Lebanon] thought we
were being 'Balkanized!' "

Then, growing serious, he notes that "Lebanonization
is interpreted—unfairly, I think—to be the conflict within
the same nation on matters which are largely sectarian or
confessional. I see the other side of the coin. Lebanonization
is the will to stand so many pressures and come out of the
confessional and national conflict."

It's a comment that speaks volumes about El Hoss's
character—his sense of the absurdity of international com-
parisons, his willingness to challenge accepted stereotypes,
and his deep respect for what he calls the "will and determi-
nation on the part of the Lebanese people to get out of this
quagmire."

That capacity to see beyond surfaces shows up, too, in
a comment that echoes like a leitmotif throughout this conversation: his clear distinction between "the legal" and "the
legitimate."

"My understanding of a global code of ethics," he explains, "would be a set of values and rules to govern international conduct based on a clear perception of the dichotomy
of good and bad, right and wrong, fair and unfair, which
would insure peace and stability and prosperity for all."

Such a code, he feels, must be predicated not simply on

a nation's own internal laws but on an agreed-upon, shared commitment to international law. "But a code of ethics cannot be a *substitute* for international law. You need constraints in a society, which can best be provided by the legislative framework of government. So international law would be essential for a good code of ethics. [But] the law is no substitute for the code of ethics, and the code of ethics is no substitute for international law. [They] should be complementary."

How do these two—ethics and the law—relate to one another? "I think international law, regardless of how it is conceived, should be inherently ethical. You can't have law which is unethical. It has to be *legitimate* to be really legal."

Case in point: international environmental laws. You cannot enact a law internationally or domestically, he says, that would "do harm to your neighbor. It is legal, but not legitimate. You can't just dump your refuse into the sea, polluting everybody else's environment. This would be legal according to your own standards, because it is enacted into law. But it is not legitimate. So proper international law that would be compatible with a code of international ethics should be based on legitimate considerations, on legitimate values."

Based on his own experience with government in what he calls "a beleaguered region," he ticks off several examples. First and foremost, he deplores what he calls "cannibalism in international relations."

By "cannibalism," he means the situation in international affairs where "the interests of the great powers prevail" not only at the expense of the smaller nations but at the expense of justice itself.

"I have come to the conclusion, after over seven years of experience at the helm of executive authority during a period of conflict, that the big powers who actually have the final say in matters relating to the world order care only for those who can do *good* or do *harm*. If you cannot do good or harm they just do not care for you."

Kuwait, he says, is a case in point. "Kuwait can do a lot of good. It has a lot of oil reserves, it provides a lot of oil on the international market, it can make a lot of investments."

"Somebody questioned whether the world would have rallied the kind of military force in the Kuwait Gulf episode if Kuwait were carrot producing rather than oil producing. The answer is obviously 'No.' So it was not a matter of justice, but rather of interest. I think it is wrong to make interests of the powers so [dominant] in governing or regulating international relations."

Too often, he continues, the world appears to be controlled by the "Machiavellian rule" that might is right. In the face of that, however, is a growing call for democracy around the world. "I think democracy is a must for all over the world. But is there enough democracy at the international level? I think there is very little of it, if any."

Democracy, he says, is "freedom of expression plus accountability plus equal opportunity. Okay, you give freedom of expression to all peoples. But can you make the big [power] accountable for everything it does at the international level?"

"The highest international authority is the Security Council of the United Nations. There you have five [countries] with veto power. They have permanent seats; they are not accountable for what they do. So what is the accountability at the international level for the big and what is the equal opportunity for the small? If democracy is to be defined as freedom plus accountability plus equal opportunity, two-thirds of it is lacking."

As an example, El Hoss cites the 1978 Israeli invasion and subsequent occupation of the south of Lebanon. Shortly after the invasion, the Security Council adopted Resolution 425—which, he says, was "very clear in its wording" in calling for the immediate withdrawal of the Israeli forces from all Lebanese territories.

"Now, fourteen years later, the 'immediate withdrawal' has not taken place, and nobody cares. Whereas in 1990 Iraq invades Kuwait and suddenly the whole world cares."

Would he be willing to talk with Israel over the Lebanese occupation? Yes, he indicates—but that's not the point.

"I agree fully that negotiations would be the best means for reaching happy conclusions for any kind of conflicts between countries. I am absolutely against violence. I don't consider it as a means [for peace but] for self-destruction. However—and this is the ethical side of it—*what* negotiations, between *whom?* Negotiations between two unequal partners would not lead to an equitable result. Because too often, you know, negotiations are a reflection of the balance of power on the ground, not a matter of forceful argument against forceful argument. We have all the forceful arguments in the world, but when you argue with someone who

280

is much stronger than you are they just ignore you. You need someone to tip the balance once in a while—or keep the balance in the name of equity."

Another reflection of cannibalism in international relations, he says, concerns what he calls "collective punishment ." Here, he turns to Lebanon itself as a case study. Just before the Iraqi invasion of Kuwait, he says, plans were afoot to raise two billion dollars to rebuild the devastated Lebanese infrastructure and economy, under a design proposed by the governments of Saudi Arabia, Morocco, and Algeria. With the outbreak of the Gulf War, however, the discussion languished. And with the end of the Gulf War, another argument arose against the reconstruction plan, to the effect that Lebanon should not be given any aid at all as long as any Western hostages were held there.

"I sympathize with this problem," he notes. "I am completely, absolutely against hostage taking, and if we had any means for releasing any hostage we would not have hesitated for one moment." But why, he asks, "punish the whole Lebanese people? These people have been punished very hard."

He sees similar problems in the case of Iraq. "I was absolutely against Iraq in their move against Kuwait. That was absolutely wrong." But he feels that to enforce an embargo against the entire nation—especially when "we knew at the time that if the embargo is strictly enforced tens of thousands of children are liable to die because of illness and hunger"—was wrong. "To punish Saddam Hussein, you punish the living. I am against that."

"What do you do? I don't know what you do, but it is

unethical that someone else should pay the price for a handful of people who have done something wrong."

Would it have been better, then, to have sent in a hit squad to assassinate that handful of wrongdoers?

Not at all, says El Hoss. "I am against the very idea. I don't go for violence at the individual level or the mass level." He observes that any such plan, if it were carried out by an agency of a government, would have to be approved, at least tacitly, at the highest levels of that government.

"I was a prime minister for seven and one-half years. I can't imagine myself signing a death penalty for anybody in the world. I think that is completely illegitimate, and I [think] that is the kind of thing a code of ethics should deal with."

El Hoss also takes a firm stand against what he calls "clandestine or illicit activities—intelligence, for instance. I think this is a good case where you have something legal but not legitimate. Every country has its own intelligence machinery. It is very well recognized, it is famous, and it is assigned huge budgets every year. They have a lot of money to dispose of, and they kill, they torpedo, they undermine. It is legal because it was established by law. But what they do is wrong and not legitimate—legal, but not legitimate."

So how could a code of ethics, he asks, "condone the existence of intelligence services in every country that kill, torpedo, and so forth?"

Another issue that El Hoss would like to see a code of ethics address is the global supply of arms. He notes that the five permanent members of the Security Council—the

United States, Britain, France, China, and Russia—are the major suppliers of arms around the world.

"Weapons become harmful only when they fall in the hands of those who abuse them or misuse them," he observes. Yet those five nations, he says, export arms to countries that *do* abuse and misuse them. "I think it is unethical for a big power to supply arms and then go to the United Nations Security Council and condemn what the beneficiaries are doing. Ethically, the big powers are responsible for all actions undertaken by those who buy arms or weapons from them. They are responsible for the arms they supply."

The arms problem raises for El Hoss yet another concern about the inequality of large and small countries, which he puts starkly. In the eyes of the large countries, he says, "small countries have no right to have any differences among their people." The reason: an internal conflict can "quickly develop into a regional and international conflict."

In a small country like Lebanon, he says, conflicts lead each party to want to be "stronger than the other" by obtaining the "instruments of power, which are money and weapons." Yet because these must be imported, "once you get money and weapons from outside, you become a vassal to the donor or the supplier." As a result, the conflict "very quickly develops into a proxy regional and international conflict."

Has the danger of proxy wars erupting out of internal conflicts been lessened by the demise of the Soviet Union as a superpower?

"One superpower might be a little better than two superpowers in conflict," he says. "But I think that we can do without any superpowers. To be a superpower in the world scene means that you can enforce anything you want, which is anathema to democracy and international relations."

With the Cold War over, he says, there is much less threat of "large wars on a large scale." Instead, El Hoss sees a future in which "the conflicting forces of powers would be economic rather than military." He sees, in fact, three economic blocks vying with each other: the North Americans, the European Community, and some of the Southeast Asian nations, with Japan included. "In such a world, he observes, "the rules of the game would change."

How will that affect the smaller nations? At present, he answers, it is clear that no progress can be made on any international issues "without the consent or approval or support of the United States. This is a fact of life. We concede to that and we accept it: whenever we have a problem we go the United States, and if we don't get the positive response, we have to suffer for it. These are the rules of the game at the present. How long this will last I don't know. The standards of power will be different later on—maybe twenty years from now, I don't know."

Yet will that create a more peaceful world, given that so many of the world's conflicts have religious, rather than simply economic or military, roots?

"I suspect that whenever the party system is not very well organized or active, the sects, or sectarian activities, supplant the parties and become parties. And this is very dangerous. In a sectarian system, your loyalty is first to your sect, because you reach where you reach because you are a member of that sect, not because of your qualifications or because you are a national of a country." In such a system, he says, the sects assume undue importance—and the potential for internecine conflict increases.

The answer, for El Hoss, is deliberately to create "interconfessional parties" which would include "a mixture of membership from all [the sects]." He has been proposing electoral laws in Lebanon, for example, that would enlarge the electoral districts beyond the geographical boundaries of the sects—to the point, in fact, of making the entire nation one electoral district.

That way, he says, if a candidate is too closely identified with any single sect, he or she will not be elected. "So you have to moderate," he says, and "cannot be a radical in your own community and be a member of Parliament any more. You have to address yourself to a larger mixture of people—a must for moderation."

Asked, finally, what he would say to the children of the future about the need for a global ethic, he emphasizes again the distinction between the legal and the legitimate. Without the legitimacy that derives from ethical action, he notes that while "you can have maybe law and order for some time," you will not have peace.

"Peace is equivalent to stability. Stability means a long-term perspective of no problems. And you can't have this unless you are having a fair deal, you are having just treatment, and so forth."

Jeane Kirkpatrick

Counting the Spoons

*I personally believe that a meaningful
international code of ethics will also affirm
human rights.*

J eane Kirkpatrick has long been something of a surprise.
A wife and mother, she made her mark as United States
ambassador from 1981 to 1985 to that most male-
oriented of organizations, the United Nations. A self-
described "Humphrey-Jackson Democrat," she became the
first Democrat appointed to a cabinet-rank position in the
Reagan administration, finally changing parties to join
the Republicans in 1985 after leaving her U.N. post. An

academician and scholar, she mastered the world of *realpolitik*—and defended the conservative global agenda so well that the delegates at the Republican convention of 1984 gave her louder and more sustained applause than Mr. Reagan himself. An early and vigorous critic of communism, she has praised Soviet President Mikhail Gorbachev for "changing the world."

Born in Oklahoma and educated at Barnard College and Columbia University, she became professor of political science at Georgetown University in 1973 and wrote *Political Woman*, a book published the next year. But it was her article in *Commentary* (November 1979) entitled "Dictatorship and Double Standards" that changed her career. In it, she criticized President Carter's administration for undermining, in the name of human rights, pro-American governments that were autocratic while smiling on totalitarian revolutionary movements. The article came to the attention of President Reagan, who appointed her as permanent representative to the United Nations in 1980.

Long known as one of the nation's most articulate conservatives, she is also a strong supporter of the women's role in public life. "My experience demonstrates," she wrote for *Who's Who*, "that it is both possible and feasible for women in our times to successfully combine traditional and professional roles, that it is not necessary to ape men's career patterns . . . but that, instead, one can do quite different things at different stages in one's life."

●　　●　　●

As she was leaving her post at the United Nations, Jeane Kirkpatrick recalls, she gave an address to her colleagues about her experiences there. "I thought very hard whether there were any values, ethical principles, which almost everybody in the organization shared," she says during an interview in her spacious office at the American Enterprise Institute in Washington. "And I remembered Samuel Johnson's story in which he told someone, 'If you really don't believe there's a difference between right and wrong, no difference between good and bad, then I say to you that when you leave my table I'll count my spoons.'"

"I concluded that we didn't steal each others' spoons. That was about the only thing I could think of that we *didn't* do, but we didn't do that. And we didn't settle disputes in the Security Council, or even the General Assembly, by force.

"There wasn't much, though, that I could find that everyone agreed about."

Part of the reason, she explains, is that, despite all the talk to the contrary, "there isn't any global community. If we use the word *community* in the sense that social scientists use it, it isn't that group of people united by shared values and goals and practices. I think there are a lot of individuals in different countries who share values. But I don't think you can speak sensibly about all the countries in the world constituting a community of shared values."

But isn't the United Nations a kind of global community?

"Look, almost nobody has ever understood my views

about the United Nations," she says. "The U.N. is not an actor—it's an arena, in which member states do whatever they want to do. The U.N. is not like a country: it doesn't have a resource base like a country. It does what the member states want it to do—want to do through it, actually."

As long as the Cold War paralyzed common action, she says, the United Nations was "not a very useful arena for most purposes. I used to say that about the only issue on which the whole world had a shared perspective and interest was something like abolishing tuberculosis." Now that the "structured divisions of the world" are changing, however, the possibilities for acting jointly through the United Nations are "greatly enhanced," as demonstrated by the concerted action over Iraq's invasion of Kuwait.

Yet even the much-touted international agreements that brought so many disparate nations together during the Persian Gulf War—seen by many at the time as a sign of shared moral concern over the fate of Kuwait—do not convince Kirkpatrick that there is, in fact, a common core of global values. Why? Because, as she says, "I know something about what you have to do to get that kind of vote."

" It isn't as though some of these countries, these representatives, just looked at an issue and reacted by saying, 'By golly, that's wrong!' Because as I'm sure you know, there has to be a good deal of persuading, of lobbying, behind those votes."

Nevertheless, she feels the vote did mark a significant change. The Soviets, she said, really did seem to respond to the Iraqi invasion "on the basis of shared principles." And that, she says, was "a very big, important difference."

"One of the absolute obstacles to common action in the period in which I was in the U.N., and I think during the whole Cold War, was that the Soviets operated from a completely different definition of aggression." Given the recent changes in superpower relationships, however, the permanent members of the Security Council are finally "operating on the basis of the same definition of aggression."

"So I think something very important has happened, and it's important for the emergence of some kind of near-global, or at least very broad, international agreement on some very fundamental values. If we can just hang on to a common conception of aggression, that's already the beginning of something important."

Prohibiting the use of force in settling international disputes, then, is for her a "desirable" element of any code of international behavior. Added to that, she says, would be a statement on human rights.

"I personally believe that a meaningful international code of ethics will also affirm human rights, very much on the Helsinki model. And I think that it would be possible to get fairly broad, nearly universal agreement in the abstract on the Helsinki values." Agreements on monitoring the implementation of those values, however, would be far more difficult, because monitoring sometimes involves "intervening in what are often very violent processes."

In addition to the shared institutional values, however, Kirkpatrick also points to a sharing of personal values—even across apparently impassable lines of political disagreement—as a central feature of a global ethic. At the United Nations, she recalls, "I think there was a kind of assumption, on the part of almost everyone, that people would help one another at the personal level." She recalls, for example, an occasion when a Soviet colleague called her at home on a Sunday afternoon "in the depths of the cold war, in the Andropov period." He began the conversation, she recalls, "by saying, 'I need your help. I want to ask a favor.' "

What he wanted, in fact, was some personal advice about getting help for a medical problem. "I don't think he had the slightest doubt that he would *get* my help," she recalls, "nor did I have a moment's hesitation about *giving* him my help."

On another occasion, she recalls, "somebody with whom I was barely on speaking terms officially called me—again on a very informal basis—to ask my advice about schools for his children. I don't think he had the slightest doubt that I would give him my very best opinion and also my assistance in dealing with that [issue]."

What does that tell her about the presence of shared values across various cultures? "It's probably significant," she notes, "that among people who had worked to- gether—even though they had largely disagreed almost all the time and didn't even necessarily trust each other to tell the truth—there was an assumption that, in interpersonal, human contacts of a personal nature, there would be a [rela- tionship] beyond political disagreements, and that you could assume decent consideration."

"That's probably significant ethically, don't you think? It's like children playing Time Out—it's as though every- body's in a role, and suddenly somebody says, 'Time out!

We'll take care of this small personal problem!' And then we agree once again to assume our roles."

Does this more interpersonal ethic arise from the increasing intercultural interaction that individuals have through nongovernmental organizations?

"It may very well," she says. She recalls Orville Freeman, former U. S. Secretary of Agriculture and a personal friend, telling her that when he became president of Business International in 1970 "he had an experience for the first time of being with people from all over the world who shared the same interests. He said it was a very different experience, with many fewer barriers, from dealing with people as representatives of governments."

"So if everybody were working for IBM, say, then they would not be separated by national identifications when they considered IBM's interests. There is a different level of internationalism working than [there is] where government is the unit. I think you're right that the multiplication of contacts of a nongovernmental sort may very well hasten the whole process of finding common interests and common values."

Turning to the Gulf War, she takes exception to those who approached the issue by asking whether this was "the right war at the right time."

"Only those who engage in a deliberately aggressive war for utterly expansionist purposes enjoy the luxury of deciding 'the right war at the right time,' " she observes. "Everybody else, certainly including the United States, is forced to react to the problems that are presented."

Given Saddam Hussein's "intransigence when confronted with the whole world's opinion of his acts," she feels
that the decision to go to war was "a reasonable response to
an unreasonable action." Nor would sanctions have worked:
there were no grounds for "supposing that he was the kind
of person who would change his policies because of depriva-
tions imposed on his people."

She is not, however, a thoroughgoing hawk. "War is
always undesirable," she notes, adding that "any resort to
force should be a very late option, never a first option."
Moreover, she says that the goal in the Middle East should
be to stem violence rather than foster it. She hopes the resolution of the present conflict will lead to "a less violent politics in the region through the discrediting of at least two of
the leading practitioners of violent politics, namely Saddam
Hussein and Yasir Arafat. If we could break the habits of
violent politics in the region, then all kinds of new possibilities for peaceable relations would open up—not only among
Arabs and Israelis but among others as well."

But is war the way to break habits of violence?

"I don't believe in 'peace at any price,' " she says, adding that peace, as an end in itself, is not "the primary value
in the United Nations charter."

"I really believe that the central value in the U.N. charter
is a world order based on states embodying respect for
human rights and democratic institutions and economic development. I think the nonuse of force is part of that, but
I don't think it stands above those [other values]. I don't
even think life is the supreme good. It's very nearly the
supreme good, but quality of life matters a lot, too. And

freedom matters a lot—prosperity, a decent standard of living, possibilities for self-development."

At the beginning of the Gulf crisis, she says, she asked herself "a lot" whether the issues there were important enough to justify war. "I finally concluded that I was willing to take [President George Bush's] judgment. Certainly Saddam Hussein was dramatically involved in behavior that was a denial of all the values of the U.N. charter."

So what were the U.N.-backed powers fighting for? "For a vision of a world in which there is no room for behavior like Saddam Hussein's," she says. She admits that there are other cases of "aggression, occupation, oppression, and brutalization" of populations—Ethiopia, for example—which have not led to multinational warfare.

The difference in this case, she notes, is the presence of oil—which, for her, is not an unworthy cause for warfare. Oil, she explains, is so important globally that "if a monopoly or even a semimonopoly position were to be developed by a man of the demonstrated intentions of Saddam Hussein, then it would be very, very dangerous for everyone." Why? Largely because he could use the vast resources of an oil monopoly to acquire "the nuclear weapons he has been systematically seeking."

"I think Saddam Hussein aspires to be the leader of the first nuclear Arab superpower. I wouldn't mind having an Arab superpower, in principle, or even a nuclear Arab superpower, if it were prepared to be a responsible member of a world community. But clearly Saddam Hussein is not going to head such a state."

In a world of Saddam Husseins, then, how important is it to have a shared code of ethics?

"I think that the same processes that make the idea of a universal, or even broadly [accepted], code of values *possible* also make it *important*."

These, she concludes, are "the processes of globalization."

Federico Mayor

A World of Crystal

Now it is time for action. We must not wait
until we can get the complete diagnosis. The
complete diagnosis is an autopsy.

He is a biochemist by training and a statesman by
choice. But these days, as the world moves through
what he calls "the turning point of history," Federico Mayor is an ethicist by force of circumstances.

Since 1987, as director-general of the Paris-based
United Nations Educational, Scientific, and Cultural Organization (UNESCO), he has repeatedly emphasized what
he has called "our common spiritual and intellectual heri-

tage—the fruits of knowledge, human rights, the universal values and principles." That has not always been easy. He came to the helm of UNESCO after the previous director, Amadou-Mahtar M'Bow, permitted such scandals that the United States, Britain, and the Soviet Union pulled the plug on funding. His task, quite simply, was to restore the organization's credibility in the face of profound skepticism.

Born in Barcelona of Catalan parents, Mayor served as minister of education and science in Spain from 1981 to 1982, and became a member of the European Parliament in 1987. A former professor of biochemistry at the Autonomous University of Madrid, Mayor has written on such topics as genetic manipulation and human rights. Not surprisingly, when 107 prominent intellectuals in 29 nations (including 11 Nobel Prize recipients) endorsed his UNESCO candidacy in 1987 "without reservation," nearly three-quarters of his supporters were from the scientific community.

In a wide-ranging interview during a 1992 biotechnology conference in Miami, Mayor noted that new global realities—the defeat of communism, the clamor for democracy, the peril to the environment, the internationalization of the economy, and the insufficiency of sovereign boundaries to contain or repel global problems—are promoting new recognitions of the need for ethics. Having consulted with more than eighty heads of state in his years as director-general—leaders whom he characterizes as individuals of "extraordinary good will" intent on joining forces to make deep changes—he feels he has discovered their central concern. It is, he says, a focus on values.

● ● ●

"We cannot only live by short-term, cost-benefit approaches. We need to provide particularly the young people with some spiritual values and committments."

The words are Mayor's. But the sentiment behind them, he says, expresses the "top preoccupation" of the world's leading statesmen.

In a world beset by economic, military, and political turmoil—and spiraling into a twenty-first century rich with new technologies—world leaders might be expected to have harder-nosed concerns. Yet Mayor expresses no surprise at their unanimity in reaffirming the underlying ethic of humanity.

"We have forgotten about the values, about the spiritual heritage and patrimony that is the only thing that can give cohesion to our prospects for the future," says Mayor. "The result has been that we are today confronted with global problems."

Not surprisingly, Mayor sees the foremost event of the age as "this wonderful moment of the collapse of the communist world." Yet he worries that the West, lacking a coherent structure of values and a clear intercultural voice, is failing to build on this moment.

As evidence, he cites the European Community, which, because it is essentially an economic rather than a cultural union, has proven "unable to cope" with the urgent demands for democracy welling up in the former Iron Curtain nations.

"We have only been spectators, not actors," he laments. The newly liberated nations of Eastern Europe, he says, were "trying to find, at the end of the tunnel, people with values. They were dreaming of democracy. They were being told [by the West], 'Welcome to our system of freedom. We will help you. We are going to assist you.' "

Yet when they were finally freed to pursue their dreams of freedom, the West let them down. "We have not reacted as humans, but only as economic individuals," says Mayor. "The only thing they found were businessmen—the free market law, not the law of equity and solidarity and human friendship.

"I always remember with immense gratitude when a president of the United States said, 'We want all the world to share the American dream'—because that is the most important thing to share, the dreams. Now I am sad, because even equity—the most important value in all the world—has collapsed. Nobody is taking care of equity, or fraternity, or freedom."

Yet those ethical values, he insists, are the essential benefit that the Western democracies must contribute to the rest of the world. "My experience as the leader of the intellectual organization of the United Nations is that today, more than ever, ethics is at the very, very forefront of the world preoccupation as we approach the next millennium."

A minority view? In a world focused on economic and political theory as the principle explanation of behavior, it may seem so. For Mayor, however, history proves otherwise. He notes that three decades of what the United Nations calls "International Development Strategy," focusing on "pure economic growth" among the less developed nations, has failed to right the world's imbalances.

"Of course, economic growth is absolutely indispensable," he says. It is, however, "not sufficient." The lack of

what he calls "development with a human face" has produced a situation in which the less developed 80 percent of
the world—known as the South, since so many of these
countries lie near or below the equator—still has the benefit
of only 20 percent of the world's resources. Although development strategy called for heavy investment of funds and
knowledge in the South, "the real situation today is that in
the two most important 'wealths' of any country—economy
and talent—the facts are the exact opposite." In 1991, he
says, "the net outflow from the South to the North was $62
billion, and the brain drain has been extraordinary."

In prior decades, that situation might have appeared tol-
erable to the North—in part because populations were
smaller, and in part because there was less intercommunica-
tion with the South. Today, however, "there are no boundaries anymore. We cannot say, 'Well, this asymmetry or dis-
parity doesn't affect us,' because it does."

What has changed? For Mayor, the answer is that today,
as never before, we live in what he calls "a world of crystal,"
where increased communication and transportation have
made barriers suddenly transparent and where actions once
hidden are now visible. Imagine, he says, gesturing past his
open balcony window toward the far wall of his hotel room,
that "in the next room one person is killing another at this
moment." It is only because the wall is opaque and because
we are ignorant, he observes, that we are not accomplices
to the crime. If the wall were crystal, he says, "we could not
say, 'Well, that's in the other room!' We would have not
only the right but the responsibility" to intervene.

Likewise, he says, in a "world village of crystal" we have

"the duty to intervene when we know that human rights are being violated in a scandalous way in a neighboring country." Failing to do so, he says, will only exacerbate the problems, which will eventually spill over from South to North.

"I am persuaded that if we in the rich part of the world are unable to knock at the door of the developing countries in the next few years, they will knock at our doors in a very loud way before very long."

Nor will the resolution of these problems be through war, as has so often been attempted in the past. His reason for describing this age as "the turning point of history," in fact, is that "for the first time we realize that, because of the immense technological progress of warfare, war is non-sense. It is completely stupid to try to protect boundaries, when boundaries do not exist any longer for pollution, for pandemics, even for money."

"We are at a crucial moment, and in this moment we pass forth from beings who can produce some local wars and conflicts [to beings who are] confronted with our responsibilities for the first time. And it is not only the responsibilities of those who are the decision makers at the governmental level."

During the cold war, the responsibility for making ethical decisions of a global scope was seen to rest on the leaders of the superpowers. Now, he says, "we also have on our shoulders the responsibility, each of us" to warn the leaders about collapsing values, failing ecological systems, and violations of human rights.

With this new primacy of individual responsibility has

come a new emphasis on democracy. Does that mean, then, that the United States and the other Western democracies should actively export democratic theories and models? For Mayor, the answer is complex.

"Democracy—like freedom, like love—is not a given. You cannot decide by decree, 'Tomorrow you are a democrat.' This is one process that is forged in each human soul and that is reflected afterwards in behavior. You must reconquer every day your life, and your freedom, and your democracy."

But that process, as the former Soviet Union is proving, takes time. However powerful the movement toward democratization launched by Mikhail Gorbachev—whom Mayor calls a "very lucid and courageous man"—the results are slow to appear. The Soviet citizenry "didn't know what private ownership was, they did not [know] what 'free market' meant."

"We must be less impatient concerning the processes," he concludes, instead of saying " 'we are democrats [today], tomorrow the results!' "

That need for patience is at the root of Mayor's concerns about the much-touted new world order. He worries that such a call for a new order—words which, he says, were first pronounced by Italian fascist dictator Benito Mussolini on the eve of World War II—overlooks the diplomatic and political tools already in place and could lead to immense frustrations.

"We already have a new order," he says. "At the national level, the name of that new order is democracy. At the international level, it is the charter of the United Nations. Let us if necessary make some adaptations—transform, even radically, the United Nations system as a whole, including UNESCO. But [let us] not again create expectations [that can't be met]. If you are not reasonably sure that you can achieve, do not frustrate people. I have seen so many people with frustration in the Eastern and Central European countries, people who for many years were thinking of democracy and now are deeply frustrated."

That frustration arises, according to Mayor, because the West is confused about how best to provide the basis for democracy to the newly liberated nations. One point is clear, however: the West cannot simply export its institutional models for governmental, educational, or financial organizations and hope that they will work. "Our models are not perfect—not at all," he says. "We must export the principles and values upon which all democracies are built, but let us refrain from always sending our models."

One such imperfect model, says Mayor, is the free market. "We talk about free markets," he says, "when we know that they are the most protected markets in the world. The protection of the agricultural markets of the European Community alone last year was around $300 billion. And we say that this is a free market! We need a conceptual review of what we are talking about."

Such a review, he hopes, will produce deep changes. But for that to happen, "we must call on the conscience of the richest in the world—not only millionaires, [but those] richest in knowledge in the privileged part of the world. We must say, 'To change, you must have some internal convictions—since you will never change if you do not want to leave at least a little part of what you have.' "

Why is change so necessary? Mayor simply points to the scale of global problems. "We cannot consider it normal that every day thousands of children are dying. We cannot consider it normal that in many countries children are educated in hate and in aggressiveness against their neighbors. We cannot consider it normal that some of the habits of the affluent society are destroying the biosphere. We must protest. We must change ourselves—and to do this, as in chemistry, we must be far from equilibrium."

"If we are not rebels, if we decline [to act because] we are already in our good comfortable chair, nothing will happen. It will be an immense frustration. [But] to the extent that we change the things of the world, we will really promote ethical values."

Mayor concedes that the promotion of ethical values sometimes runs into deep resistance. That, however, arises from a confusion between what he calls "political feelings or beliefs" and the "essential values" that underlie humanity's ethical framework. "Nobody can oppose [the idea] that children must be educated in freedom and love and equity," he says. But in recent years, he notes, people have seemed afraid to talk about such deep individual values as love—a fear he traces, in part, to the influence of "the kind of uniformity that was imposed in some countries" by the Marxist-Leninist theories. In addition, he says that "professors and teachers sometimes transmit their own political feelings" instead of basic ethical values. "This is dishonest," he insists. "Education is precisely the moment in which you must provide each person [with the ability] to express his potential according to his own wishes. A free person is one who is able to act according to his own views and to his own perceptions."

Given such confusion, can humanity ever arrive at a common core of values? Yes indeed, says Mayor. "There are a lot of fundamental values that are reflected in the Universal Declaration of Human Rights that nobody opposes." The challenge is to understand these values quickly enough to arrive at common answers to global problems. "For the first time in the history of mankind," he notes, "we have in our hands the possibility of producing irreversible damage to our ecological conditions. So today, for the first time, there are some actions that only now can be taken, but must be taken now."

Perhaps the largest obstacle to timely solutions, he says, is that "we are always making new reports. I think that most of the diagnoses have already been made, and now it is time for action. We must not wait until we can get the complete diagnosis. The complete diagnosis is an autopsy."

Is the world capable of such wholesale change? Mayor is an optimist—although he resists using that word, quipping that an optimist is sometimes nothing more than a pessimist who lacks good information. "I am a hopeful person," he says, largely because of his great faith in the internationalism that originally brought the United Nations into existence in 1945 after the "immense horror and compassion and passion of the Second World War."

Now, as then, is a time for "new breakthroughs," he concludes. "I think we must create [again] this kind of human intervention. And this is only possible with spiritual values."

SEVEN

Values for Humanity

If the moral threads of the preceding interviews are traced, untangled, and rewoven, the tapestry they form illustrates our common ethical ground. The eight values mentioned in the first chapter and discussed at greater length below constitute a global code of values. Not *the* code, but *a* code. The process used here, after all, is not meant to produce the only set of values upon which wise men and women around the world could reach consensus. It relies too much on subjective judgments and intuitive assessments, rather than scientific weightings and sample analysis. Some day, perhaps, social scientists using sophisticated survey techniques will pull together a statistically valid statement of global core values. This book, while pointing toward the values they may find, makes no pretense in that direction.

To say that, however, is not to dismiss the process used here. A number of very important things in life—from a newspaper's deadline story on a political revelation to the choice of your marriage partner or your religion—also depend on intuition and subjectivity. Most of us wouldn't have it any other way. But most of us also want some assurance that the judgments are sound and the assessments valid.

The validity of this code depends on four factors. First, obviously, is the choice of interviewees. Only to the extent that these voices speak with the resonance of their own cultures will they articulate a set of shared and deeply rooted values. And only to the extent that the mix of interviewees covers a spectrum of backgrounds, regions, and persuasions will the selection be balanced and representative.

The second factor involves the honesty and depth of the conversations. As any experienced interviewer knows, a line of questioning can readily be arranged so that the responses fall into a predetermined pattern and support the hypothesis at hand. Even more dangerous is the questioner's accepting as a profound statement of conviction what the interviewee has intended only as a passing comment, or the short-circuiting of a discussion without exploring the nuances within the ideas.

The third factor concerns the care with which the conversations are reported. Not having a transcript of the actual interview, the reader has no check on the accuracy or completeness of the original statements. Even more difficult is the problem of context: every quotation has a setting, consisting not only the words immediately surrounding it but the rivulets of ideas that came to the surface fifteen minutes earlier, disappeared underground, and then bubbled to the surface once again.

These three factors shape any piece of reporting. How well the reporter handles them determines, in large part, the trust established between reader and reporter. In theory, each factor is subject to verification—by comparing the interviewees selected to those available but unchosen, or by consulting the notes, transcript, or recording of the interview for questions asked and answers given. In practice such verifying is rarely done. Most readers either trust the writer or stop reading.

Since trust is implicit in any sort of reporting—especially in a book about values—every effort has been made in this study to observe carefully the imperatives of these three factors. But a fourth factor figures here that, because it shows up less commonly in journalism, deserves more comment: the process of analysis. The method here consisted of a careful reading of the preceding chapters with an eye to locating the essential moral values that most interested the interviewees. These values were listed on a large piece of graph paper, using words drawn from the interviews themselves. In the end, some sixty-five terms appeared down the vertical axis, ranging from such broad and widely shared concepts as *responsibility* and *tolerance* to such specific ideas as *curiosity* and *the collapse of central authority*. The names of the interviewees were listed horizontally across the top. Wherever one of the interviewees identified the concept as a strongly held core value, that fact was noted with a double check mark at the appropriate intersection on the graph paper. If the concept was mentioned in passing, but still with some degree of emphasis, it warranted a single check mark.

Adding up the checks was easy: *respect for life* got thirteen, *love* got eleven, and so forth. Spotting commonalities was harder. When James Baker spoke of *the right to differ from authority,* was that close enough to what Oscar Arias and John Gardner meant by their emphasis on *individual conscience* to be lumped into one overarching category? It seemed so, and it further seemed that *liberty* and *freedom* also belonged there. In another area, *love* seemed to embrace the ideas of *compassion, charity, helping one another,* and *honor.* Once such conflations had been made, a tally of the check marks pointed fairly clearly toward the eight values listed here.

Subjective? Certainly. Replicable by others? To some extent, yes: any reader of these interviews, with pen in hand and a good-sized sheet of paper, should come pretty close to the results here. Valid? Probably, in that this eight-point code of values bears striking resemblance to lists of values derived by participants in numerous ethics seminars conducted recently around the United States by the staff at the Institute for Global Ethics. This is not, in other words, an off-the-wall, unique, bizarre list. It may even strike us as familiar, ordinary, and unsurprising. That's a comforting fact. Codes of ethics, to be practicable, need to have behind them a broad consensus. The originality of the list matters less than its consistency and universality.

In an ideal world, one would have assembled all the

interviewees around a table, had each talk for an hour, had each listen intently to all the others, and finally had them arrive at a consensus. If they could have done so, here's what they might well have agreed upon.

• *Love.* Despite the concern of James Joseph in Washington that "the L word, love" is falling sadly into disuse, it figures prominently in these interviews. "Love, yes," says Astrid Lindgren in Stockholm. "This is the main word for what we need—love on all stages and with all people."

"The base of moral behavior is first of all solidarity, love, and mutual assistance," says Graça Machel of Mozambique. Shojun Bando in Tokyo agrees, detailing three different kinds of love and insisting that "It shouldn't be that *others* should tell you to love others: it should just come of its own will, spontaneously." Or, as Nien Cheng from China puts it, "you cannot guide without love."

For Reuben Snake of Nebraska, the central word is compassion. "We have to be compassionate with one another and help one another," he recalls his grandfather telling him, "to hold each other up, support one another down the road of life." Thinking back on her dealings with a global spectrum of cultures at the United Nations, Jeane Kirkpatrick in Washington notes that, no matter how severe the political differences, "there was a kind of assumption, on the part of almost everyone, that people would help one another at the personal level."

• *Truthfulness.* Of the four theses on former Harvard president Derek Bok's code of ethics, two center on truth. "You should not obtain your ends through lying and deceitful

313

practices," he observes, and you have a "responsibility to keep [your] promises." Astrid Lindgren puts it with equal clarity when she speaks of the need to "be honest, not lying, not afraid to say your opinion."

Looking through the lens of science, Kenneth Boulding of Colorado also puts "a very high value on veracity—telling the truth. The thing that gets you run out of the scientific community is being caught at telling a lie." Fortunately, says Muhammad Yunus of Bangladesh, the spread of technology makes it increasingly difficult for truth to be hidden. In the future, "people will be forced to reveal themselves," he says. "Nothing can be kept hidden or secret—not in computers, not in the halls of government, nothing. People will feel much more comfortable when they're dealing in truth. You converge around and in truth."

Here, however, as with many of these global values, there is also a residue of concern—a fear that trust, which is central to honesty and truthfulness, seems to be falling into abeyance. "The idea that you ought to be able to trust somebody is out of fashion," worries Katharine Whitehorn of London. That's a point seconded by James Baker of Indiana. "Little by little," he says, "if we let that trust go out of our personal dealings with one another, then I think the system really begins to have trouble."

• *Fairness.* Elevating the concept of fairness or justice to the top of his list, John Gardner of Stanford University says that "I consider that probably the Number One candidate for your common ground." By *justice*, he means "fair play, or some word for even-handedness."

"Here one could get caught up in the very complicated theories of social justice," warns James Joseph. "Or one could simply look at the Golden Rule. I relate fairness to treating other people as I would want to be treated. I think that [rule] serves humanity well. It ought to be a part of any ethic for the future."

For many, the concern for fairness goes hand in hand with the concept of equality. "The pursuit of equality is basic," says Sergio Muñoz of Mexico City and Los Angeles. "The people who come from Mexico and El Salvador have the same values, in my point of view, as the person that comes from Minnesota or from Alabama or from California—those basic principles that are common to all civilizations." For Muñoz, as for A. H. Halsey at Oxford, equality stands as one of three legs underpinning the French Revolution's motto of liberty, equality, and fraternity.

For some, like Joseph, the concept of fairness and equality focuses strongly on racial issues. Others, like Jill Ker Conway from Australia, see the need for "greater equity between the sexes." Still others, like Federico Mayor of Spain, see the problem as one of international relations: despite the groundswell of interest in democracy arising within the former East Bloc nations, Westerners "have not reacted as humans, but only as economic individuals. . . . Even equity—the most important value in all the world—has collapsed."

• *Freedom.* Very early in human history, says John Gardner, "the concept of degrees of freedom of my action—as against excessive constraints on my action by a tyrant or by military conquerors—emerged." Even the earliest peoples "knew when they were subjugated"—and didn't like it. That desire for liberty, he says, persists to the present as one of the defining values of humanity.

But liberty, many say, requires a sense of individuality and the right of the individual to express ideas freely. "Without the principle of individual conscience," says Oscar Arias of Costa Rica, "every attempt to institutionalize ethics must necessarily collapse. . . . The effect of one upright individual is incalculable. World leaders may see their effect in headlines, but the ultimate course of the globe will be determined by the efforts of innumerable individuals acting on their consciences."

Such action, for many of these thinkers, is synonymous with democracy. "I think democracy is a must for all over the world," says Salim El Hoss of Lebanon. He defines the ingredients of democracy as "freedom of expression plus accountability plus equal opportunity." While he worries that the latter two are lacking in many countries, he notes that the first condition, freedom of expression, is increasingly becoming available to "all peoples."

• *Unity.* As a counterbalance to the needs of individual conscience, however, stands the value that embraces the individual's role in a larger collective. Of the multitude of similar terms used for that concept in these interviews—*fraternity, solidarity, cooperation, community, group allegiance, oneness*—*unity* seems the most encompassing and the least open to misconstruction. For some, it is a simple *cri de coeur* in a world that seems close to coming undone. "I want unity,"

316

says Dame Whina Cooper of New Zealand, adding that "God wants us to be one people." For Varindra Tarzie Vittachi of Sri Lanka, the idea of unity embraces a global vision capable of moving humanity from "unbridled competition" to cooperation. "That is what is demanded of us now: putting our community first, meaning the earth first, and all living things."

The problem, says Father Bernard Przewozny of Rome, arises when the common good is interpreted "by seeing the relation between the individual and the common in individualistic terms." Carried to that extreme, he says, individualism is "destructive of social life, destructive of communal sharing, destructive of participation," adding that "the earth and its natural goods are the inheritance of all peoples."

• *Tolerance.* "If you're serious about values," says John Gardner, "then you have to add tolerance very early—*very* early. Because you have to have constraints. The more you say, 'Values are important,' the more you have to say, 'There are limits to which you can impose your values on me.' "

"It is a question of respect for the dignity of each of us," says Graça Machel. "If you have a different idea from mine, it's not because you're worse than me. You have the right to think differently." Agreeing, Derek Bok defines tolerance as "a decent respect for the right of other people to have ideas, an obligation or at least a strong desirability of listening to different points of view and attempting to understand why they are held."

"You have your own job, you eat your own food," says Le Ly Hayslip. "How you make that food is up to you,

317

and how I live my life is up to me." Without that sense of tolerance, she says, "we create a big problem for others."

Reuben Snake traces the idea of tolerance back to a religious basis. "The spirit that makes you stand up and walk and talk and see and hear and think," he says, "is the same spirit that exists in me—there's no difference. So when you look at me, you're looking at yourself—and I'm seeing me in you."

Abstracting from the idea of tolerance the core principle of respect for variety, Kenneth Boulding links it to the environmentalist's urgency over the depletion of species. "If the blue whale is endangered, we feel worried about this, because we love the variety of the world," he explains. "In some sense I feel about the Catholic church the way I feel about the blue whale: I don't think I'll be one, but I would feel diminished if it became extinct."

• *Responsibility.* A. H. Halsey places the sense of responsibility high on his list of values—because, he says, of its impact on our common future. "We are responsible for our grandchildren," he explains, "and we will make [the world] easier or more difficult for our grandchildren to be good people by what we do right here and now." It's a point made in a different way by Katharine Whitehorn, who notes that while as a youth "it's fun to break away," it's very much harder to "grow up and have to put it together again."

For Nien Cheng, the spotlight falls not so much on the actions of the future as on the sense of self-respect in the present. "This is Confucius' teaching," she says. "You must take care of yourself. To rely on others is a great shame."

But responsibility also demands caring for others, says

Hayslip. Under the complex interactions of medicine, insurance, and law that exist in the West, however, "If you come into my house and see me lying here very sick, you don't dare to move me, because you're not a doctor. So where is your human obligation? Where is your human instinct to try to save me? You don't have it. You lost it, because there are too many rules."

Yet paradoxically, says Oscar Arias, "responsibility is not often mentioned in discussions of world politics or ethics: there, the talk is all of rights, demands, and desires." Human rights are, he says, "an unquestionable and critical priority for political societies and an indispensable lever for genuine development. But the important thing is not just to assert rights, but to ensure that they be protected. Achieving this protection rests wholly on the principle of responsibility."

Chicago attorney Newton Minow agrees. "I believe the basic reason we got off the track was that rights became more important than responsibilities, that individuals became more important than community interests. We've gotten to the point where everybody's got a right and nobody's got a responsibility."

At its ultimate, this sense of responsibility extends to the concept of the right use of force. "You shouldn't perpetrate violence," says Derek Bok simply, finding agreement with Jeane Kirkpatrick's insistence that "war is always undesirable" and that "any resort to force should be a very late option, never a first option."

• *Respect for life.* Growing out of this idea of the responsible use of force, but separate from and extending beyond it, is a value known most widely in the West from the Ten

Commandments: Thou shalt not kill. For Shojun Bando, it is an inflexible principle: even if ordered in wartime to defend his homeland by killing, he says, "I would refuse. I would say, 'I cannot do this.' "

Such an idea, expressed in today's peaceable Japan, may seem almost naive when examined through the lens of such war-riddled areas as the Middle East. Yet Salim El Hoss takes much the same view. "I was a prime minister [of Lebanon] for seven and one-half years. I can't imagine myself signing a death penalty for anybody in the world. I think that is completely illegitimate, and I [think] that is the kind of thing a code of ethics should deal with."

Reuben Snake, noting that the Indians have a warlike reputation, notes that "probably the most serious shortcoming of tribal governments is their inability to effectively resolve conflict within the tribe and externally." He describes earlier Indian traditions, however, in which great efforts were made by the tribal elders to prevent killing. That's a point with which Tarzie Vittachi—himself from the much-bloodied nation of Sri Lanka—feels perfectly at home. The first element of the Buddhist "daily prayer" under which he was raised, he recalls, is " 'I shall not kill.' " It is also central to the Ten Commandments of the Jewish decalogue under which Newton Minow was raised and that he still feels form the basis for the world's code of ethics.

•

There are, of course, other values that surface strongly in these individual interviews. Nien Cheng, for instance, points to courage. "One should basically know what is right and what is wrong," she says, "and, when you know that, be courageous enough to stand for what is right." Figuring strongly in Shojun Bando's pantheon is wisdom, which he defines as "attaining . . . detachment, getting away from being too attached to things." Whina Cooper puts hospitality high on her list, recalling that her father said, " 'If you see any strangers going past, you call them—*Kia Ora*'—that means to call them to come here." Astrid Lindgren puts an emphasis on obedience—a quality that runs throughout the life of her most famous character, Pippi Longstocking, though usually in reverse. Kenneth Boulding points to peace, which he defines simply as "well-managed conflict." Thinking of peace brings Salim El Hoss to the concept of stability. "Peace is equivalent to stability," he says, adding that "Stability means a long-term perspective of no problems." These and other values, while they don't find broad support, have firm proponents in these pages and deserve serious attention.

Another set of issues also arises regularly within these pages: the burning public concerns for racial harmony, respect for women's place, and the protection of the environment. Many of the interviewees touch on them, and some elevate them to high priority. Speaking of the need for racial harmony, James Joseph puts at the top of his list a sense of "respect for . . . the cultures of other communities, respect for the need to begin to integrate into our collective memory appreciation for the contributions and traditions of those who are different." Jill Ker Conway tops her list with a warning about the "increasing exploitation of women" she sees around the world. And of the many human rights identified by Father Bernard Przewozny, the one to which he has dedicated his life is the "right to a healthy environment."

These three issues don't figure on the final list of core values. That, however, does not make these crosscutting and overarching themes insignificant. They are not *values* as much as *goals*—two terms that, along with the words *plans* and *tactics*, need defining and distinguishing if we are to understand the relevance of this code of values to the problems facing us in the global tomorrow. So much confusion arises over these terms, in fact, that it may be worthwhile to offer some clarification.

By *values* we typically mean, as the *Oxford English Dictionary* confirms, those qualities that are "worthy of esteem for [their] own sake" or have "intrinsic worth." Used by itself and in the plural, the word usually suggests *moral* values, where moral (from the Latin *mos, moris,* meaning *manner, custom, habit, way of life, conduct)* pertains to whatever is right, proper, and good. Values need to be distinguished from *goals*, which, according to a wonderfully garrulous 1926 *Merriam-Webster Dictionary,* is "the final purpose or aim" or "the end to which a design tends, or which a person aims to reach or attain." And goals need to be distinguished both from *plans*—the broad outline of action leading to the attainment of the goal—and from *tactics,* which embrace the specific details whereby the plan is to be put into operation.

These distinctions are most helpful if the four terms are seen to occupy four descending levels. Values, topping the ladder, are the stuff from which real vision is made. At the bottom are tactics, through which practical, hands-on change occurs. Between them are the intermediate steps—the goals articulated to reflect the values, and the plans laid down to reach the goals. It is in a confusion over those four concepts that leadership so often comes apart. How? Quite often by emphasizing tactics over values. As a friend likes to observe, that's a bit like asking a road map, "Where should I go?" rather than, "How should I get where I already know I want to go?" It's asking for vision from something only capable of giving direction.

A surprising amount of what passes for leadership is bedeviled by this confusion, which creates two difficulties. The lesser difficulty is that people invest mighty efforts at the wrong level of activity. The greater difficulty is that, ignoring the power of shared values, groups fragment and antagonize over tactical disputes. It's probably fair to say that much of the gridlock and frustration in democratic political processes around the world arises from an emphasis on tactical over values-conscious thinking.

The eight core values articulated here represent the highest rung on the visionary ladder. How do we know they ought to be in that top spot? Because they all flunk the "Why" test. If you ask of any tactic, "Why do that?" the answer will usually come back that "It supports the plan." If you ask, "Why this plan?" the answer will be in terms of the goal: we do *this* because we want to get *there*. Ask "Why this goal?" and you're apt to get a value: we want to stamp out cheating because we believe in truthfulness. But ask "Why does truthfulness matter?" and the answer will either be a slack-jawed stare of amazement that anyone would have to ask, or an extended and complex metaphysical discussion touching on God, man, and the nature of good and evil. To be sure, there is something above the top rung—a most important philosophical inquiry—but it's not part of the ladder.

If these eight core values stand on the top rung, the three crosscutting issues identified above—involving race, women, and the environment—occupy the second rung, where the goals stand. Why does racial harmony matter? Try tolerance, or fairness, or freedom. Why should we care about women? Think about love and unity. Why be concerned about the environment? How about responsibility and respect for life. The fact that we can so readily answer the *why* suggests that these three are not, in the end, core values. It also suggests just how important these issues are: you cannot fully embrace this code of values without being forced, sooner or later, to come to grips with these and other major, first-intensity issues of our time.

So what good is this code of values? It gives us the way to build downward to the level of goals, plans, and tactics, where things really happen and the world really changes. It unifies us as we move around on the ladder, giving us a home territory of consensus and agreement. And it gives us a way—not *the* way, but *a* way—to reply when we're asked, "Whose values will you teach?" Answering this last question, as we tumble into the twenty-first century with the twentieth century's sense of ethics, may be one of the most valuable mental activities of our time.

Index

•

327

Nations: internal conflict in, 283;
small versus powerful,
278–279. *See also*
Superpowers
Native Americans. *See* American
Indians
Nesbitt, Prexy, 88–89
North-South inequity, 135–136,
303, 304

O

Obedience, 232, 321
Oil, 295
Oneness, 316; as future basic
ethic, 146–147; global, 3–4;
Maori emphasis on, 112;
Snake on, 32

P

Patience, 172
Peace, 321; Boulding on, 159;
Hayslip on, 71; as stability,
285
Philanthropy. *See* Charity
Phung Thi Le Ly. *See* Hayslip, Le
Ly
Plans, 322
Population growth, 224
Poverty: Arias on, 263, 272;
freedom from, 148–149; in
Mozambique, 89, 95;
prevalence of, 224
Power, use of, 232
Priorities: in American and
Japanese business, 176; in
public spending, 104–105
Problem solving, global, 9–11
Promiscuity, Buddhist prohibition
on, 220
Prosperity, and religion, 59
Przewozny, Father Bernard, 3,
73–83, 317, 322

R

Racial equity, 164–165
Racial harmony, 321
Racism, 39
Rankin, Robert, 36–37
Raven, Peter, 74
Reagan, Ronald, 264, 288
Relationships: Confucian
teachings on, 209; as ethic in
business, 171; need for,
219–220
Relativism, 14–15; Bok on, 101;
and science, economy, and
technology, 77–80; in
universities, 123–124
Religion: commonalities in, 127;
of Cooper, 114–115; as global
ethics basis, 80–81; Japanese
interest in, 58–59; and
prosperity, 59; as source of
ethics, 45–46; superstition as,
153; as system of relationships,
220. *See also* Buddhism;
Christianity; Islam
Respect, 265, 267–268; for
others, 38–39; Snake on, 27
Respect for life, 19, 312,
319–320; Bando on, 54–55;
Machel on, 95
Responsibility, 19, 311,
318–319; Chinese sense of,
207–208; as future common
ethic, 122–123; individual,
304–305; toward
environment, 82, 83; as value
for next century, 265,
266–267; versus right,
182–185, 319
Rhodes, Frank H. T., 98
Right and wrong: instilling, in
children, 214; knowing, for
survival, 213, 215; lack of
distinction between, 181–182